Principles and Processes of Music Education

NEW PERSPECTIVES

Principles and Processes of Music Education

NEW PERSPECTIVES

MALCOLM TAIT
Case Western Reserve University

PAUL HAACK
University of Kansas

Teachers College Press, Columbia University
New York and London   1984

Published by Teachers College Press, 1234 Amsterdam Avenue, New York, N.Y. 10027

Grateful acknowledgment is made to the following for permission to reprint previously published material.

United Press International: UPI Press Release in *Times–Sun*, Kotka, Finland, November 9, 1981.

Library of Congress Cataloging in Publication Data

Tait, Malcolm, 1933–
  Principles and processes of music education.

  Includes bibliographical references and index.
  1. Music—Instruction and study. 2. School music—
Instruction and study. I. Haack, Paul, 1935–
II. Title.
MT1.T13   1984   780′.7   83-18031

ISBN 0-8077-2756-3

Manufactured in the United States of America

89 88 87 86 85 84   1 2 3 4 5 6

Contents

Preface

What is music education and where does it derive its essential qualities and characteristics? If we are involved with music education, or wish to be involved, we have to understand how music and education come together and how they interact and combine to assist human growth. This book is based on the belief that music and man *can* interact in very special ways, but for this to happen man must meet music purposefully, in an educational atmosphere. While casual interaction may yield some positive and pleasing effects, carefully planned interaction through education can bring about profoundly beneficial and deeply satisfying results. It is this carefully planned interaction that should characterize music education. The interaction becomes the experience and the experience is the heart of the educational process.

What happens to us when we experience music? We certainly hear sounds, but if the experience stops there, it is difficult to explain why we return time and again to our favorite compositions. There is more to a musical experience than merely hearing. The nature of this "more" is of central concern to music education.

Most people agree that the basic purpose of education is to prepare people for worthwhile, rewarding living experiences. It follows that music education prepares people for worthwhile and rewarding musical experiences. We could say that for this to happen, we need to encourage discriminating listening or skilled performance, but to stop there is to ignore the fundamental importance of human involvement in the musical experience. In music education we need to be very sensitive to the nature of human involvement with sound, for it is a process that is sometimes objective, orderly, and predictable, and at other times highly subjective, imaginative, and mysterious. When music is experienced in an educational environment, obviously there should be increased *musical* understanding, but, in fact, understanding cannot occur without an increased sense of *self*-awareness and fulfillment. In order to facilitate this we need a clear idea of how music and man interact with one another. Such understanding then provides the basis for effective music education and its vital components, the processes of planning, teaching, learning, and evaluation. And that is what this book is about.

Accordingly, what follows is a contemporary text that constantly strives to emphasize consistency and congruency between principles and processes in music education. Our intent is a text in which the proposed practices of music education are firmly grounded in and consistently developed from fundamental principles based on the nature of mankind, music, and education.

Part I provides succinct reviews, as well as our views concerning the nature of man, music, and education. These are explored to reveal basic points of congruency, which in turn yield basic principles for a consonant theoretical framework. In part II we build on this framework a proposal for music education methodology that relates consistently to the basic objective of all education, enhanced human development. Thus what this text offers is a fundamental viewpoint that is extended as consistently as possible into a proposal for the effective practice of modern music education.

We have developed the text as a whole and in its various parts to serve as a basis for introduction to music education, principles and general methods classes, as well as for use in graduate foundations and advanced methods courses. Such multiple functions are possible because the text sets forth a novel and broad framework, within which teachers and students operate and elaborate to fill in the details based on the fundamental ideas and the general examples provided. Also, the text is not designed to be definitive in any specific realm of the music curriculum. Rather we have proposed basic ideas for and employed examples drawn from the various curricular approaches and levels of music education. Again this provides working room for the creativity of the teachers and students who use it so that they may generalize or make specific applications in light of their own needs and purposes.

Each chapter is introduced by a brief list of "Underlying Concepts," which are in effect the hypotheses that provided the bases for our reasoning. These are presented at the outset to provide students with our rationale for the ideas developed in the chapter. In plain words, we want the students to know where we are coming from. As "advance organizers," these succinct statements offer a germinal overview and also may serve as introductory discussion topics or as material for concluding critiques. Interspersed at appropriate points throughout each chapter are suggestions for class activities and discussions. These are designed to extend thought and stimulate action along topic lines. They also may serve as examples or generative ideas for more particular activities and discussions relevant to the specific time, place, and purpose for which the book is being used.

We have provided a section entitled "Extensions" at the end of each chapter. These series of statements, questions, and suggestions for action are intended to extend the ideas already presented within a chapter, and may be used independently outside of class time. However, a teacher may wish to introduce ideas from "Extensions" into class discussions when they seem relevant and valuable.

Each chapter concludes with a list of references and readings that offer additional background and insights into the chapter content from both historical and contemporary perspectives. These may provide bases for further study as desired.

It is highly recommended that students keep a journal while they are studying this text. The journal should reflect personal reactions and reflections concerning the materials presented in the text and in class. In the context of the journal, selected statements, questions, and action suggestions within "Extensions" can form the basis of an ongoing personal dialogue between individual students and the teacher. The purpose of the journal is to challenge students to consider issues in depth and to express opinions in a developmental record that can reflect originality and growth in the ability to reason and to communicate fundamental principles and processes of music education. A teacher may expect several entries each week and may want to review and add comments to journals at one- or two-week intervals. One particularly effective arrangement is what might be called a "double double-entry" procedure. In this case the student uses two journals, on an alternating basis. Thus while the teacher has one for review and comment, the student is working in the other and vice versa.

By way of general introduction, we readily acknowledge that, in our effort to provide a comprehensive foundation and a contemporary orientation to the field of music education, we have based our novel contributions on the work and experience of many other scholars and practitioners, past and present. What we have intended is not so much a different as an expanded, holistic view of music education; one which will be serviceable for young persons who will face the challenges and opportunities of the approaching twenty-first century and its rapidly developing soundscapes.

The generative point of the text is our belief that the truly well-developed human being, the man or woman "for all seasons," is one who thinks carefully, feels deeply, shares generously, and thus acts wisely, humanely, and socially. The unique nature of mankind evolves from man's extraordinary capacities for thinking, feeling, and sharing in a social, culture-inducing manner; and this is the point of chapter

1. Chapter 2 examines the nature of music and the ways in which music is congruent with the nature of man—the ways in which musical behavior can enhance and enrich human behavior. The third chapter deals with education as a means of strengthening the effective range and depth of interaction between man and music. Education, the pivotal aspect of part I's discussion of principles, leads us to the second part of the text, which is concerned with four activities or processes basic to effective music education.

Thus, principles lead to processes, and foundational viewpoints concerning man, music, and education yield the procedural bases for providing essential educational activities. Teaching, learning, planning, and evaluation are considered in turn, and cumulatively as interacting operations.

Simply put, with this text we are attempting to help teachers help students realize their human-musical potential. Music can be a highly satisfying, human need-fulfilling experience: Because it emanates from the life process, it can also serve as a powerful model to illuminate and enliven that process. In its various aspects music develops our thinking, feeling, and sharing abilities, the very behaviors in which we find our greatest human potential. Our educational behaviors must be consistent with the nature of man and music, and that is the basic concept this text hopes to facilitate in practice.

PART I

Principles of Music Education

Principles: Beginnings; foundations; origins; sources; essential aspects; ultimate bases or causes; fundamental assumptions; beliefs exercising direct influence on life; rules of conduct consistently directing behavior; that from which things proceed . . .

The basic music education processes of planning, teaching, learning, and evaluating must proceed from *principles* that relate directly to the essential nature of man, music, and education. Only these sources can provide the legitimate foundations and directions for music education methods that foster human development and human living in the richest sense.

In keeping with these beliefs, we devote chapter 1 to an examination of the unique nature of mankind, emphasizing those extraordinary and distinguishing human capacities for thinking, feeling, and sharing, those capacities that provide the potential for musical behavior in particular and for a truly well-developed human being in general.

In chapter 2 we present views of the nature of music as it relates to and emerges naturally from the nature and needs of mankind. Here we focus on the congruity of musical and human experience; indeed, on the unity of musical and human behavior.

This leads quite naturally to chapter 3, where we view education as a catalyst for bringing man and music together. Via effective education, music can become a highly satisfying, need-fulfilling reality, as well as a motivational model and means for the nurturing of well-rounded human beings and quality life experiences. Education is viewed as the primary avenue and music as the primary vehicle for fostering the clear thinking, deep feeling, and generous sharing that elevates the quality of human life.

In simplest terms, effective music education brings together man, the subject, and music, the object, in a rich variety of subject-object interactions designed to enhance human living and human development. Such subject-object relationships, along with the experiences and insights they yield, are vitally useful, essential, and fulfilling throughout our lives.

Thus we take the view that musical behavior is a natural and vital part of the life process, and, to be effective, processes of education must be congruent with the processes of life. So, "principles," beliefs, and fundamental assumptions about man, music, and education provide the ultimate bases for the rules of conduct and the behaviors inherent in a consistent, logical teaching-learning process. Part I of the text is meant to provide such bases for the "processes" that follow in part II.

1

Man

Underlying Concepts: The life process is about human development and the realization of human potential; and thus it is about growth and maturity and all that comes between. . . . Musical processes are analogous to life processes, and thus can be revealing, useful, satisfying, and valued.

The living process at its most fundamental level embodies characteristics common to all people, places, and times. The qualities of these characteristics influence the qualities of the living process.

The ability to identify basic human characteristics and needs such as music and to translate them into one's personal value structure plays a significant role in determining the quality of individual and social living.

A primary characteristic of the "whole human" is the ability to relate one's inner world of feeling, thinking, and imagining to the outer world of social sharing.

Films and television programs that introduce visitors from other galaxies have become immensely popular. The entertainment industry has made vast capital by contrasting outer space beings with earthly human beings in a series of programs that often have been provocative, exciting, or at least amusing. Many of our human behaviors, customs, and qualities have been satirized in very clear and intriguing ways; we have been amused to see ourselves reflected as robots or amazed to realize that much of what we take for granted is apparently difficult for "visitors" to comprehend. This entertainment phenomenon provides an excellent point of departure for us to examine the nature of man and of human behavior.

Before departing, however, it should be absolutely clear that we regard a consideration of the nature of mankind as the essential, the only real and valid starting point upon which to base subsequent considerations of musical and educational behaviors and practices. Without a human foundation and context, the study of music and education becomes as "unreal" as some of the other-worldly creatures encountered in the aforementioned dramas. So now, let us go on.

If we were suddenly confronted with some visitors from space who wanted to prepare a documentary report about human existence on earth for dissemination to their fellow beings, what would we tell them; what would we show them; and on what bases would we make our selections? Would we, for example, embark on a tour of the great artistic masterpieces of the world; the cathedrals and temples, the museums and concert halls, or would we show our visitors some of the beauties of nature at the Grand Canyon, the Himalayas, the Grecian isles, or the African veldt? Perhaps we would wish to schedule a visit to the United Nations General Assembly, the British Houses of Parliament, or Capitol Hill in Washington. On the other hand we may wish to point out the vast hydroelectric dams, the aircraft factories, the nuclear reactors, or the oil refineries. What about the schools, the universities, and the libraries; and how would we explain our kitchen gadgets, washing machines, automobiles, clothing, food, housing, and so on? Perhaps we could let them read a newspaper, but in what language, and would we want them to read the crime reports, the business section, the fashion news, the international page, the arts reviews, sports, advertising, or the weather?

Which of man's physical, social, or cultural achievements would you wish to share with our astro-visitors and what are the bases for your selections? Which currently performed musics might be most revealing? Why?

The choice is indeed staggering and a whirlwind tour of places and events might provoke more questions than answers. Tourists tend to see only superficial things for the most part because they are rarely in one place long enough to begin to grasp cause and effect; so we would need to consider the rationale for our tour package very carefully. A smorgasbord approach would serve to illustrate different flavors but it would not necessarily demonstrate the relationships between the flavors or even why certain flavors exist. We would probably wish to give our visitors the impression that our itinerary as well as our behaviors were more than a series of haphazard and unrelated events. To do this we would need to be as clear as possible about the reasons for including some things rather than others.

One approach to this problem might be to separate the phenomena that have to do with the physical world *external* to man, from the *internal* world of the mind. At first glance this may seem ideal and we could embark on our tour of the Grand Canyon, the veldt, and the Himalayas; but this would serve only to illustrate man's environment, indeed, to an extent, only man's unmodified environment. On the other hand, it could be argued that a visit to our schools and universities would illustrate events more directly related to the mind.

Let us suppose that our visitors, having viewed some of the natural physical environment as well as a formal learning environment, would move on to see how man lives. They might expect to see some direct relationships between the physical environment, the learning environment, and the resulting life style. In other words, they might reasonably expect to see connections between what is learned in school and how we live out of school.

> Discuss some examples of direct relationships between what you have learned in school over the years and things that you do out of school. Can you think of some areas of your life where you wish you had had additional learning opportunities in school? Why?

Such connections would be more apparent in some areas than in others. For example, our schools have taught us how to improve our health, how to strengthen our buildings, how to increase our farming and industrial outputs, and how to speed up communications. Examples of direct relationships between what is learned in school and the mastery of our physical environment abound and our visitors would surely be impressed with the range of these examples.

The sense of power, mastery, and control that mankind has developed over the external environment is nothing short of fantastic. There now exists a high-technology superstructure, the basis of much of our power, that surrounds and at times dominates us; that provides a cushion of health, wealth, entertainment, and security. Although the benefits of this technological revolution are not equally distributed among all people, most countries and societies have felt its impact to some extent.

If our visitors were to return to their own galaxies at this point, their documentary report would probably evoke some envy and admiration for the human species on earth. However, if they decided to probe a little deeper, they might find other human qualities and characteristics that are more difficult to describe and more difficult to explain. Visitors who probe further may want to know about our seemingly crime-laden cities, our strikes and demonstrations, the climbing suicide rate, drug abuse, mental illness, and social malaise.

"Are these the inevitable consequences of external strength, power, and prosperity?" they may ask. They see many human beings living lives of lonely luxury; beings who are bored while they are entertained and afraid while they are free. They see contradictions and inconsistencies between external images and self images; they see human beings adrift without direction or fulfillment; they see unconsummated lives, and they want to know why.

Do you agree with the analysis that many people are "living lives of lonely luxury"? What are some of the contradictions you have observed between outward appearances and inner truths?

The answers they would receive would not help a great deal because they are so varied. The conditions are blamed on governmental inefficiency, poor education, moral turpitude, commerical exploitation, and the demise of the family, to name just a few answers. Some of our more perceptive visitors would be quick to realize the futility of attempting to apportion blame; they recognize what exists and they also would recognize the necessity of returning to basic questions about the human kind: Namely, what is possible and what is desirable? They would argue for a more rigorous evaluation of human potential and encourage a drive toward that goal.

If we focus on potential what do we find? We find human beings who are capable of rigorous and finely structured *thinking*; beings who can respond with deep *feeling*. In combination, these factors provide the potential for social, *sharing* beings, beings whose humanity and fulfillment spring from a desire to communicate and a willingness to give of themselves, of their abilities and possessions, to an extraordinary degree. Let us consider each of these fundamental qualities in turn.

THINKING

One of man's primary goals has been to analyze critically his surroundings, the materials, the structures, and the elements that comprise them, and having done so, to expand, build, and consolidate his place in those surroundings. This after all is a basic part of a child's growth pattern. Children observe, explore, and evaluate their universe just as Pythagoras, Leonardo da Vinci, Galileo, Newton, and Einstein did. Our physical or external world has been traversed, measured, documented, and assessed and the process is still going on. We have been fascinated by our surroundings and we have brought the finest powers of our intellect to bear on attempts to interpret and understand them. We have learned a great deal in the process, knowledge and insight that has allowed us to move beyond survival to build systems that define a culture and bring a measure of quality to living. While we have spent enormous amounts of time and energy thinking about our environs, we have not spent as much time in thinking about our inner lives and the determinants of our interactive human behaviors. Even though the social and physical sciences have defined many new frontiers and provided many new insights into human behavior, widespread self-knowledge is surprisingly still in its infancy, and to this extent the human species remains somewhat of an enigma.

> The arts are among the few long-standing disciplines concerned essentially with self-knowledge. What are some others? Even in the arts, however, thinking in terms of externals seems easier than thinking about internal matters. Attempt to describe such externals and internals.

To think about events and phenomena that are external to ourselves can involve a degree of logic and objectivity that is not possible in considering the inner self. Indeed, no clear or commonly accepted definition yet exists to explain the thinking process itself. This is certainly due in part to our limited understanding of the brain and its enormously complex functions. However, we do have a vocabulary to describe many processes that to a greater or lesser extent relate to thinking. These processes include remembering, analyzing, relating, perceiving, conceptualizing, deducing, and synthesizing. Some people also include imagining, dreaming, creating, or inventing and yet others include contemplating, meditating, or praying. Certainly these are behaviors known to us all but the precise location of their operation remains uncertain. This is a problem for biomedical engineers to resolve; it is more important for us at this time to recognize the variable range of thinking processes than to know the seat of their existence. It is important for us to consider the entire range of thinking behaviors, how frequently they occur, and how we might assess their qualitative worth.

Thinking behaviors range from rigorous and focused at one extreme, to vague and spatial at the other. For example, we are all familiar with the decision-making process in a variety of areas so let us suppose we wished to take an afternoon drive in the country. Some of us would think through the whole experience before leaving the garage, that is, we would employ detailed linear and analytical thinking. Others would jump into the car and drive off with only the vaguest idea about direction, distances, and times involved. The term "spacey" is not altogether inappropriate for the latter kind of thinking! This example provides for a flexible thinking process with either extreme being possible, depending on the kind of goal or the kind of afternoon we wish to experience. Not all tasks are flexible in this way, however; some situations by their very nature call for analytical thinking while others call for more imaginative and creative thinking;

some situations require a comfortable balance of linear and spatial thought including components of analysis, synthesis, and meditation. Music, as we shall see later, is one such case.

Generally, human beings have not made significant attempts to match particular thinking processes to particular tasks or experiences; rather, they have tended to discover their own ways of thinking based largely on trial and error. This approach has probably left a residue of unrealized potential in many instances because it may never have occurred to some people to vary their ways of thinking with certain situations. Indeed, there is no way of knowing how many people sense frustration or failure in their work and their daily lives because their range of thinking is underdeveloped or inflexible.

Our schools have been criticized for their emphasis on linear, analytic thinking which, of course, has produced an abundance of linear analytic knowledge and linear analytic behavior. Schools have also been criticized for their apparent unwillingness or inability to develop creative, imaginative, synthetic, and spatial thinking, thus producing people who have unrealized creative and imaginative potential. Perhaps this is one of the reasons why many people are bored even when they are being entertained; their own creative and imaginative thinking processes are apparently not involved. Similarly, analytic thinking without the balancing force of synthetic thought produces people who, it has been said, "know more and more about less and less." Such a condition of imbalance must inevitably lead to uncertain and even precarious circumstances of instability.

Are the criticisms mentioned above valid for the music curricula that you have experienced thus far in your lives? What types of thinking should be fostered or emphasized in that curricular area?

If our thinking potential allows us to experience a wide range of thinking behaviors, then it must surely follow that, in order to be fully human, each of us should be familiar with that range and receive guidance in its appropriate use. We should, for example, come to understand which ways of thinking are most productive for us; we may find ourselves knowingly employing one way of thinking more frequently than another because that particular method produces hoped for results and makes us feel good about ourselves in the process. On the other hand, at times we may find ourselves usefully employing several thinking procedures in order to come to grips with one particular situation.

Because human potential exists for development on several fronts, it follows that qualitative thinking is most likely to be characterized by linkages between different thinking modes. If analytic thinking can be supported by intuitive, deductive by creative, logical by meditative, and linear by imaginative, then it seems likely the resulting decisions will be most favorable to the human condition. Outcomes will be balanced and holistic rather than expedient or simply efficient.

You have probably all experienced a decision-making process in which you considered all the logical and analytic ramifications of a situation, but you decided to "sleep on it" before coming to a final decision. Meanwhile, your imaginative, intuitive, and meditative thinking processes grappled with the problem and came up with an answer that was quite different from the purely logical one! How many decisions would be different if we employed a broader spectrum of thinking?

A good starting point to find answers to this question is simply to make a conscious effort to involve a variety of thinking processes when we make decisions, even little decisions like deciding whether or not to take an umbrella; whether or not to spell the previous whether "weather"; to have an extra serving of dessert; to extend a term paper; or on a somewhat larger scale to buy or not to buy a new car; to become engaged to a particular person; or to be a music educator!

> Think of an area of your life in which you have employed predominantly analytic, logical, deductive thinking procedures. Now think of an area where creative, intuitive, and synthetic thinking procedures tended to dominate. What might be some of the results if these two processes were reversed?

FEELING

The location of human feelings within the mind and central nervous system is no more clearly determined than the location of the thinking processes. Indeed, we know considerably less about feeling than we do about thinking, but no one questions the existence of feeling as a powerful life force and this is sufficient justification to warrant further examination of the subject. The range and intensity of human feeling is undoubtedly immense. It can serve either constructive or destructive ends in shaping one's self and one's self image. (Of course, the same is true of thinking processes.) There has been an underlying fear and uncertainty about discussing feelings in schools, homes, and society at large, perhaps because feeling processes have seemed to be more private and personal than thinking processes. In any event, as psychiatry has developed, human feeling has become recognized as a most significant determinant of human behavior, and accordingly more research is being done in this area.

Feeling is often considered to be an awareness and experiencing of our sense of being. We are concerned therefore with the whole range of human feeling, the frequency, the intensity, and the qualitative worth of feeling as it relates to the larger picture of human behavior.

List six feelings that you experience fairly frequently. Now list three feelings that you would most like to experience and three you would least like to experience. How many of the latter six are on your original list?

If we were to take particular note of how our feelings varied over a period of time, perhaps a day or two, we would probably find an array similar to the following: lonely, confused, delighted, calm, lazy, surprised, tense, angry, cool, and confident. There is no particular order to these feeling states. We may have an underlying disposition or set which varies more gradually than our surface feelings and which channels them to some extent in its own course; however, for the most part, our most obvious feelings simply represent responses to a variety of stimuli, a variety of situations and events that affect us in these particular ways. Indeed, it is extraordinary how much more haphazard and relatively unstructured our feelings generally are than our thoughts. Most of us order our thinking in some fashion but our feelings seem by comparison to be relatively unstructured and perhaps at times unmanageable.

Sometimes feelings tend to cluster in groups such as surprise, excitement, and joy, or tension, anxiety, and anger; and they may follow one another in rapid succession. On other occasions, one particular feeling such as loneliness or confidence or confusion may prevail for extended periods of time as an underlying factor that influences the nature of more momentary surface feelings. Some theorists such as Plutchick (1980) speak of "primary" feelings such as anger, anticipation, joy, acceptance, fear, surprise, sadness, and disgust. Others like Gaylin (1979) see feelings as being related to basic human needs and conditions. Feeling guilty, anxious, ashamed, or proud are considered to be feelings directly related to survival; whereas feeling upset, tired, bored, envious, or used are caution or stress signals. Gaylin argues that success is often heralded by feeling moved and feeling good.

Some feelings occur quite frequently. For example, most of us feel tired within a day's cycle, or surprised, delighted, disturbed, nervous, or determined. These are feelings which are relatively well known simply because we experience them on many occasions and in many situations. By contrast, some of our rarer feelings are more intense. Feeling inspired, agonized, helpless, outraged, stunned, or violent are all highly concentrated feelings. We do not usually experience such intensity of feeling frequently or for protracted periods of time.

Can you think of musical examples that are modeled on or follow
these patterns of lengthier, repeated periods of mild effect, and
briefer periods of more intense stimulation?

Intense feelings more often than not are the result of specific
special events rather than more routine day to day happenings. Intense and powerful feelings that are related to specific events are
difficult to handle because they invade and infringe on our thinking
ability, and thus may dominate our behavior.

Sometimes we describe feelings as being deep or shallow rather
than intense or mild; so that a deeper feeling than frustration might
be despair, whereas a deeper feeling than happiness might be rapture.
Then there are the negative and positive feelings, particularly as they
apply to the self-image. Feeling depressed, suspicious, confused,
hopeless, or exhausted are generally considered to exert an unfa-
vorable influence on individual growth whereas feeling confident,
relaxed, interested, energetic, or organized characterize conditions
that are ripe for personal growth and fulfillment. Then there are
those in-between, ambivalent feelings that, depending on the particular situation, might turn out positive or negative. These include
feeling challenged, excited, tense, worried, nervous, or pressured.

Are there any specific pieces of music that tend to awaken positive, negative, or ambivalent feelings in you? Do they have any
identifiable musical characteristics or associative factors that seem
to stimulate any of the specific feeling types discussed here?

We would all prefer to experience more intense positive feelings
than intense negative feelings but our lives provide us with both from
time to time. Major problems arise when there is an imbalance between these extremes. If the range of feelings is suddenly narrowed
to become intensely negative, our life support systems are going to
need additional help; or, if we find a confusion of positive and negative feelings happening simultaneously, or in close juxtaposition, we
are also going to need help. For example, we may feel great enjoyment
in participating in some event but also feel great remorse at the same
time. If these conditions continue without rationalization for extended periods of time, problems are likely to occur.

A negative and a positive experience can vary from person to
person, or even from time to time with the same individual,
depending on circumstances that surround the original feeling
state. List what are for you three very positive and three very
negative feelings. Are they always so? Are they the same for
others in your class?

As we live out our lives, we experience an extraordinary range
and intensity of feelings. We generally enjoy the high points, but

sometimes feelings are resented as interruptions or embarrassing remnants that are best forgotten as quickly as possible. The spontaneous or fragmentary nature of some feelings makes them difficult to integrate into the total fabric of life; and for that reason we have often attempted to repress or tended to forget all but the most intense, thereby missing valuable opportunities for self-understanding and growth.

Perhaps the greatest problem with feelings is their closeness to the events that create them. We can usually put time and distance between ideas and events and this allows us the objectivity to think, to organize and clarify those ideas; but feelings remain so intimately connected to their source that it is difficult to develop an underlying rationale for their existence or a sense of continuity and structure. In order to create the psychic distance and space in which to understand and learn from our feelings we need a degree of abstraction. This is provided by the world of art where feelings may be formalized, idealized, and heightened to yield valuable models, insights, and satisfactions.

Art deals with memories of feelings and imagined feelings, rather than feelings per se; it deals with feelings removed from specific events, thereby providing space in which to build artistic structures that teach and enthrall. That is why every culture and every civilization has found in art a means for identifying and understanding its most elusive and profound feelings.

John Blacking (1969) makes the point that if we regard the full development of the sense of being as a proper and legitimate aim of man's development, elevated thinking-feeling aesthetic-artistic experiences should not be regarded as abnormal or mystical. "But it is more usual to regard as normal and real the daily experiences of life, in which only a part of man's being is expressed in social and cultural forms. If these external forms become within themselves the end of man's existence, clearly man becomes alienated because he lives only a part of the reality of his whole being." Blacking adds that "the value of music lies in its power to restore and develop man's sense of being and to close the [thinking, feeling, sharing] gap that the acquisition of culture has made between the inner and outer man" (pp. 70–71).

SHARING

If thinking and feeling are essentially internal-interactive processes, then sharing is the basic external-interactive process. It is the natural outgrowth of a just combination of effective thinking and feeling. Sharing represents man's social commitment by recognizing his

individual uniqueness within a community and his willingness
to contribute that uniqueness to the community. Of course we do
not have to search far in order to document the complexity of
our contemporary communities compared with earlier forms of
social organization; and today some of our sense of sharing
has been dulled, primarily by very strong pressures to compete.
Great emphasis on competition has threatened and truncated social
sensitivity.

As long ago as the early 1940s social psychologist Eric Fromm
(1941) diagnosed a loss of individual autonomy and the adoption of
a self that could be more socially competitive. He felt that the negation
of the real self in favor of a synthetic or cosmetic self, one that appears
to succeed socially but really fails personally, had become symptomatic
of our times. In fact, in recent decades noted authors, playwrights,
artists and composers have created works on this "American Dream"
theme (e.g., Tennessee Williams's play *Night of the Iguana* and Robert
Indiana's painting *The American Dream*).

> It may be helpful to consider and discuss how several specific
> pieces of music reveal or relate to this phenomenon of the *Amer-
> ican Dream*.

Fromm (1941) argued "the loss of the self has increased the necessity to conform, for it results in a profound doubt of one's own
identity" (p. 280). Conformity, according to Fromm, is initiated when
a child begins to give up the expression of his or her feelings and
this eventually leads to giving up the feelings themselves. Ironically,
conformity often is interpreted as the epitome of social behavior,
when in effect it may not entail any significant contribution at all; on
the other hand, developing and sharing one's unique feelings, un-
derstandings, or abilities may be social behavior of the highest sort,
yet not recognized or appreciated as such.

> How real is this sense of self-alienation for you? Are you con-
> scious of having given up some kinds of feelings in order to be
> more socially acceptable or more successful in a competitive sit-
> uation? If so, when were you first aware of this?

More recently Christopher Lasch (1979) wrote that "the American
cult of friendliness conceals but does not eradicate a murderous competition for goods and position; indeed this competition has grown
more savage in an age of diminishing expectations" (p. 124). Lasch
(1979), like Fromm, argues that competition is tied to emotional manipulation and to an enormous pressure to consume as a palliative
for all ills. He believes that by surrounding ourselves with "goodies
that glitter" we cushion ourselves against ourselves. Those internal-
interactive processes we examined earlier in this chapter can then be

ignored or anaesthetized (as in antiaesthetic, unfeeling, insensitive) while the relentless drive to compete and succeed continues.

Can music be used for such purposes—as a "goodie that glitters and anaesthetizes," and for "emotional manipulation"? If so can you identify some specific instances and examples? Then consider also the role music plays in commercials and in the popular culture in general vis-à-vis pressures to consume and conform. Are consumption and conformity necessarily positive types of social, sharing behavior?

Currently there seems to be a strong tendency for people to become more and more alienated from themselves and thus from those around them. Indeed, Lasch argues that an advanced industrialized society "requires a stupefied population, resigned to work that is trivial and shoddily performed, predisposed to seek its satisfaction in the time set aside for leisure" (p. 224). To the extent that this may be true, such conditions do not make for the social behavior, the sharing behavior required to keep a people or society vital and developing.

Bettelheim (1980) echoes these thoughts when he writes, "We keep our children alienated from work achievement where it counts, and frustrate them with the semblance of autonomy by letting them decide on their course of studies, only to rob them of autonomy where it counts by putting them into the straight-jacket of an overly competitive educational and social system" (p. 346).

Alienation from self tends to lead to increased submission to external authority with concomitant feelings of individual depression, boredom, hopelessness, and insecurity. These are real feelings, deep seated and profound, feelings that can haunt people through life to an unfulfilled and resentful old age. Even if the diagnoses of persons such as those cited here are only partially accurate, there is a need for urgency in addressing the problem. Of course, our own times and conditions are always the most difficult to assess; but regardless of whether our current vacillations from the path of humaneness are momentary or momentous, serious thought and action are warranted.

If you concur with any or all of these assessments, what would be the first several steps you would take to improve our situation? Would music figure in your plans? According to Gaston (1968, chap. 1), music, because it is rooted in human experience and communicative of that experience, provides self-knowledge as well as the self-esteem that accompanies competent performances and creative activities (including listening). Can music and/or music education also be diverted to lesser purposes—to bring about over-conformity rather than creativity, to manipulate and control behavior rather than provide for expressive freedom? Consider and discuss several of the positive and negative social aspects associated with this powerful medium.

Individual worth and the values of creativity require constant reaffirmation to prevent social stagnation. We need to know ourselves and to feel good about ourselves so that self-knowledge and self-esteem can be shared and thus lead to greater knowledge of and esteem for one another. This is the basis for social well being from which democratic, economic, political, and aesthetic-artistic structures ultimately derive their validity. Some priorities clearly need rethinking so that man instead of being manipulated and controlled by his social condition remains free to discover and define his uniqueness within it.

Clearly competition is here to stay; it is a prerequisite for free enterprise in a democratic society and a valuable form of motivation for the advancement and enhancement of society in general; but it need not and should not pervade and dominate every aspect of our lives. It must be balanced with other qualities that do not automatically equate "success," and particularly success over others, with happiness.

Blacking (1969) argues that because advanced technology has increased the division of labor in many societies, the potential and real need for cooperation has increased as well. He feels that "if the potential has not been realized, it is because societies have mistakenly assumed that a division of labor must be accompanied by a division of people" (p. 67). Certainly false divisions and the fruitless, needless competition they foster represent retrogression rather than progress for humanity.

E. Thayer Gaston (1968), like many others, stressed that the emergence of cooperative sharing behavior was a prime factor in the development of humanity: Over time, the ability to channel or "long circuit" stimuli through increasingly complex brain structures, rather than simply responding with "knee-jerk" or fist-flailing reflexes, gradually led to reflective thought processes and the suppression of hostility. Thus emotions became softened and more controllable, and this allowed for the development of positive interpersonal relationships involving highly social expressions such as music. Music still communicates expressions of good will and the "tender" emotions more than any others.

Gaston drew support from Masserman, Montagu, Murphy, Allport, Leakey, Washburn, Dobzhansky, Hulse, and Harlow among others, in concluding that the trend in the evolution of humanity and culture always "has been toward greater interdependence of individuals, more communication, and those closer relationships that are characteristic of culture" (p. 12). The evolutionary development of

more "brain processing" potential between the time a stimulus is received and a response is made has allowed for the before mentioned
moderation of hostility, and for more thought controlled, mediated
reactions. This has resulted in human cooperation and the social
sharing of abilities essential to the development of culture. This same
development made possible and in fact made necessary communications systems such as speech and music which emanate from and
in turn sustain culture.

As a sociocultural phenomenon music grows out of the cultural
matrix, being bound by and representative of it. Thus music can
communicate to alleviate loneliness, even when one is alone. We need
the nonthreatening closeness to others, the feelings of belonging, the
integration with our society, the relationships and communication
with our fellow humans that music provides, even if no one else is
physically present while we interact with it and share in it.

Probably the most rewarding experiences in life occur when we
share feelings and thoughts with others. They may be simple everyday
interactions or they may be intimate and deeply moving experiences,
but when we share, we are no longer alone; generally, we can understand and enjoy ourselves more fully in a context of sharing with
others. What is musical composition, performance, and listening, if
not this?

Unfortunately the kind of sharing that is envisaged often does
not take place until some crisis sweeps into view; but sharing should
be more than just a crisis, emergency, fragmentary, or casual exchange. Sharing needs to be a regular part of an ongoing and integrated living process; a process that incorporates a broad range of
well-balanced thinking and feeling behaviors; behaviors that clarify and
build a self image that is creative, loving, and stable; a self-image that
values man's physical-spiritual wholeness and provides nourishment
for the development of a well-integrated personality which is indeed
worth sharing.

BALANCE

Achieving a balance and wholeness in human behavior and values
has been a primary but elusive goal of mankind throughout history.
The history of Western civilization is permeated with evidence of
vacillating values, cycles, and at times pendular overswings that have
resulted in highly distorted views of the nature of human beings.
Some of our historical eras are considered to have been quite "thinking" oriented, as contrasted with the "feeling" emphasis found in
other eras. The "thinking" eras tended to emphasize the more formal,
linear processes and products, as reflected in the forms of govern-

ment, economics, music, literature, drama, dance, art, and architecture associated with them. Carried to an extreme, a lack of feelingful balance could prove dangerous to the well-being and development of mankind. Of course, the opposite overemphasis on highly subjective and nonlinear processes and products could lead to chaos as well. Any student of history could point to some examples of such times.

> The following are some dichotomies that relate to the nature of mankind. Expand the list—be creative.
>
> > Thinking/Feeling
> > Rational/Emotional
> > Objective/Subjective
> > Contemplative/Experiential
> > Reason/Action
> > Form/Content
>
> Now consider further the consequences of being too one-sided. George Szell, longtime conductor of the Cleveland Symphony, reportedly said a conductor should think with the heart and feel with the brain. What did he mean? List eras and representative persons (musicians as well as others) that were exemplars and exponents of (a) thinking-oriented existence, (b) a feeling emphasis, and (c) a more balanced or holistic emphasis.

Will Durant (1977) stressed the belief "that life depends on an adjustment of order and liberty, a mutual collaboration between them and any emphasis on one or the other is destructive." His appeal is for reasonable balances and interactions between control and freedom, thought and feeling, self and sharing; and his caution is that any overemphasis on any extreme is dangerous. It seems obvious that without reasonable order and control, liberty and freedom may fall victim to chaos. Karl Pribram (1963) put it this way: creativity and freedom are rooted in a *wealth* of rules and orderliness. Real freedom is intelligent, knowledgeable choice that develops out of order when order achieves sufficient complexity.

So we need to be concerned about well-integrated, balanced, and holistic human development. Feeling without thought yields only amorphous affect; for example, in one of his songs, David Gates of "Bread" sings about life being only emotions passing by—all feeling and never understanding why (Gates, 1973). Yet without feeling there is no stimulus for thought, thought that in turn enhances and elevates feeling to a meaningful state. And without self there is nothing to share, but, in sharing, both the self and others become better known. A holistic philosophy seems essential.

The diverse and fragmentary nature of our society at this moment in history poses a real challenge for those who would seek wholeness. We may appropriately recall Blacking's (1969) comment about the mistaken assumption that division of labor must be accomplished by a division of people. Many cults exist, attesting to the numbers of people who are desperately seeking answers to their thwarted dreams and lives, often by resorting to extremes of behavior. There is abundant evidence that such problems are the result of limited vision and the imbalance between or downright denial of some of man's most humane qualities.

First, our *thinking* often has been based too exclusively in analytic processes at the expense of intuitive, creative, and synthetic processes. This seem particularly true of the training in thinking which is received in our contemporary schools. Second, our *feelings* too frequently have been stifled or over-channeled into "acceptable" behaviors at the expense of spontaneous and deep feelings. Third, our *sharing* has at times been depersonalized and suffocated by a competitiveness that has undermined and impaired vital human communications.

Consider for a moment the fact that we have had our government take over responsibility for numerous areas of social concern. The result has inevitably been depersonalization of human interaction and loss of personal communication, personal sharing. While such governmental actions may be warranted, necessary, and desirable in large and complex societies, must the interpersonal aspects be sacrificed in the process so that the "haves" and "have-nots" never interact, communicate with, or understand one another? Never really think of, feel for, and thus never really personally share with one another? Are there ways to compensate for these spin-offs of depersonalization and demoralization? Consider further that music is one of mankind's basic needs, proved so by the fact that it is found in all times and places. Discuss whether music, as a broad or basic social need, could be taken over by a government agency "for more effective dissemination and use." What would be the advantages and disadvantages of such an arrangement? Has this already happened to any extent in our society? In other societies? With what results?

In response to such conditions we are challenged to work for the development of well-rounded, integrated personalities in which thoughtful feeling and feelingful thought lead to well-informed caring and sharing behaviors. Music and music education, as we shall see in ensuing chapters, can play an enormously important role in man's development as a thinking, feeling, sharing, humane being.

EXTENSIONS

Statements

1. "What I wish to stress is the fact that since music is created by human beings, we must regard the sources, or raw materials, first of all as human facts. For it is not rhythm and sound as such but their nature as human facts which concern us." Sessions, Roger, *The Musical Experience of Composer, Performer and Listener* (New Jersey: Princeton University Press, 1950), p. 11.
2. "Art is the only means by which we can communicate both the fact and the feeling about the fact." Cary, Joyce, *Art and Reality—Ways of the Creative Process* (New York: Doubleday, 1961), p. 23.
3. "The artist in our day does not play nearly so vital a part in public life as he has done in many former ages. . . . The decay of art in our time is not only due to the fact that the social function of the artist is not as important as in former days; it is due also to the fact that spontaneous delight is no longer felt as something which it is important to be able to enjoy." Russell, Bertrand, *Authority and the Individual* (London: George Allen and Unwin, 1949), p. 48.
4. "In the course of reaching adulthood, a person's emotional and conceptual processes become more and more intimately interconnected. It is impossible to separate the two; they form a circular process. The emotional accompaniment of a cognitive process becomes the propelling drive not only toward action but also toward further cognition. Only emotions can stimulate man to overcome hardship of some cognitive processes and lead him to complicated symbolic interpersonal and abstract operations. On the other hand, only cognitive processes can indefinitely extend the realm of the emotions." Arietti, Silvano, *Creativity: The Magic Synthesis* (New York: Basic Books, 1976), p. 92.
5. "The split between thought and affect leads to a sickness, to a low-grade schizophrenia, from which the new man of the technetronic age begins to suffer. In the social sciences it has become fashionable to think about human problems with no reference to the feelings related to these problems." Fromm, Erich, *The Revolution of Hope* (New York: Harper and Row, 1968), p. 42.

Questions and Suggestions

1. How would you define human potential? How does it and how should it relate to formal education?
2. What is there in the experience of music that makes for the fulfillment of self?
3. What does man's love of music tell us about the nature of man?
4. To what extent does music help you to discover your own identity? How? What does your answer say about the nature of music in a community?
5. Why do people become involved with music? What happens to you when you become involved with music? What parts of us does music satisfy? What kinds of music does each of us relate to most naturally? How do

we account for the individual differences in the musical experience?

6. What questions if any do you ask when you are confronted with a work of art? Is there an order to those questions?

7. Do you consider yourself more re-creative than creative? What kinds of things would you do if this perception were reversed?

8. What words would you use to describe your various thinking procedures? Would you describe your range of thinking as being widely variable depending on the kinds of challenges you meet or do you tend to apply one or two thinking procedures to most situations?

9. To what extent is "goodness" related to likes and dislikes? Can we be fair to those things that are contrary to our taste?

10. What is the nature of the musically mature person? Does he or she accept a plurality of artistic standards?

11. Has art become less or more human as it has become more available?

12. How can we share our feelings nonverbally? Can you communicate an idea, image, or feeling without using words? Try working in pairs to communicate qualities of feeling and qualities of movement.

13. Can a society be both sensitive and efficient?

14. For a difficult but informative exercise, try to note your feelings as you go through one to two hours of your daily routine. Do you believe that in general your feelings are less structured than your thoughts? Are your feelings more spontaneous than your thoughts? Do you have difficulty separating the two?

15. Do you believe your life has been enriched by artistic experiences? If so, can you recall several specific instances?

16. In some cultures funeral "celebrations" are times of sadness for the loss of a fellow human being; but the ceremonial ritual and music and the affiliated food and drink may be enjoyed with great exuberance. Are there situations such as this in our society? Is this good or harmful? To what extent does the effect/affect seem to depend on the customs and mores of the culture or sub-culture?

17. How would you define musicality or musical talent? Collect three different definitions from different sources and compare them with your own definition.

18. Describe the nature of a peak experience. How can you share such an experience? Should you try? Is that what education is about?

19. Explore the relationships between the democratization of art on the one hand and the dehumanization of art on the other. What are the implications for music education?

20. Discuss how much of yourself you are sharing in your musical performances. Are you sharing just those aspects of yourself you feel most confident about, or are you sharing your total image of yourself?

REFERENCES AND READINGS

Arietti, Silvano. *Creativity: The Magic Synthesis*. New York: Basic Books, 1976.
Bettelheim, Bruno. *Surviving and Other Essays*. New York: Vintage Books, 1980.

Blacking, John. *How Musical Is Man?* Seattle: University of Washington Press, 1973.

Blacking, John. "The Value of Music in Human Experience." *1969 Yearbook of the International Folk Music Council.* Urbana: University of Illinois Press, 1969.

Blakeslee, Thomas R. *The Right Brain.* New York: Anchor Press/Doubleday, 1980.

Bronowski, Jacob. *The Ascent of Man.* Boston: Little, Brown, 1973.

Choate, Robert A., ed. *Music in American Society: Documentary Report of the Tanglewood Symposium.* Washington: Music Educators National Conference, 1968.

Clynes, Manfred. *Sentics: The Touch of Emotions.* New York: Doubleday, 1974.

Dobzhansky, T. *Mankind Evolving.* New Haven, Conn., Yale University Press, 1962.

Durant, Will. Interview published in the *Topeka Capitol–Journal,* December 4, 1977, p. 21.

Fromm, Eric. *Escape from Freedom.* New York: Avon Books, 1941.

Gallwey, W. Timothy. *The Inner Game of Tennis.* New York: Random House, 1976.

Gaston, E. Thayer. "Man and Music." In *Music in Therapy,* edited by E. Thayer Gaston. New York: Macmillan, 1968.

Gates, David. "Baby I'm-a Want You," from the recording tape *The Best of Bread.* Elektra Records, 1973.

Gaylin, Willard. *Feelings, Our Vital Signs.* New York: Harper and Row, 1979.

Hall, James B., and Ulanov, Barry. *Modern Culture and the Arts.* New York: McGraw-Hill, 1967.

Lasch, Christopher. *The Culture of Narcissism.* New York: Warner Books, 1979.

Maslow, A. H. *The Farther Reaches of Human Nature.* New York: Viking, 1971.

Maslow, A. H. *Toward a Psychology of Being.* Princeton, N.J.: Van Nostrand, 1962.

Montagu, Ashley. *The Humanization of Man.* Cleveland: World Publishing, 1962.

Murphy, Gardner. *Human Potentialities.* New York: Basic Books, 1958.

Ornstein, Robert E. *The Psychology of Consciousness.* San Francisco: Freeman, 1972.

Plutchik, Robert. *Emotion: A Psychoevolutionary Synthesis.* New York: Harper and Row, 1980.

Polanyi, Michael. *The Study of Man.* Chicago: University of Chicago Press, 1958.

Pribram, Karl H. "The New Neurology: Memory, Novelty, Thought, and Choice." In *EEG and Behavior,* edited by G. H. Glaser. New York: Basic Books, 1963.

Sagan, Carl. *The Dragons of Eden.* New York: Random House, 1977.

Samples, Bob. *The Metaphoric Mind: A Celebration of Creative Consciousness.* Reading, Mass.: Addison-Wesley, 1976.

Sudnow, David. *Ways of the Hand.* Cambridge, Mass.: Harvard University Press, 1978.

Zuckerkandle, Victor. *Man the Musician, Sound and Symbol: Volume Two.* Princeton, N.J.: Princeton University Press, 1973.

2
Music

Underlying Concepts: Music processes and life processes are closely analogous and can be mutually supportive. In effect, music is a life analogy that yields valuable insights and opportunities to explore the experience of living.

Music may be experienced as a continuum from objective acoustical phenomena to subjective psychological experiences. It can be thought-provoking, feeling-provoking, or a combination of both. Because music is a sociocultural phenomenon, it is also a sharing experience, even when one is performing it or hearing it alone.

Musical meanings are a product of what a person brings to music as well as what he or she takes from it. Meanings, functions, and values are all closely related and interdependent.

There is a well known round that begins with the words: "Music is everywhere under the sun. . . ." Today we could add "and the moon," for indeed in this day and age it is difficult to find silent space for any extended length of time. We are surrounded with music in stores, elevators, airports, factories, and on beaches. Furthermore, the variety of musical stimuli has never been greater. At the mere flick of a switch we can hear vast libraries of music from rock to pop, opera to symphony, music from Africa or Asia, and music that is sacred or secular or anything in between. We have musical environments of staggering proportions.

We also find music being employed to serve an extraordinary number of different functions. Religious music is no longer the exclusive domain of the churches; in fact, the great body of religious music is probably now heard more frequently in concert halls, on car radios, or on records in people's homes than in the context of the religious services for which it was originally composed. Similarly, chamber music is no longer restricted to concerts or palaces, or folk music to intimate gatherings in village squares. Perhaps even more significantly, music of one culture, whether it be from New Guinea or Peru, has become part of a grand category of world musics. Increasing concern for and interest in world musics have provided a paradise of sounds for ethnomusicologists to document and describe, and an ever-increasing wealth of music for public stimulation and consumption.

Much music has been associated with particular locations and/or functions, but is now being adapted to fulfill new functions in a rapidly changing world. Music is being utilized for such diverse purposes as advertising, baby-sitting, marketing, agricultural production, and therapy. We have music to soothe and music to stimulate, music for youth and music for old age; we have dinner music and elevator music, music for this place and that; for these events and those; we have, it seems, music for times of the day, days of the year, and seasons of our lives. In fact, we have so many musics we are sometimes confused as to what is and what is not music!

In several countries, dairy farmers use music to enhance milk production and some hog farmers know that suitable music at feeding times, generally of a sedative type, seems to help the animals gain weight more quickly. Other farmers have discovered that the growth of some plants such as corn can be accelerated by playing stimulative types of music so as to enhance capillary action and soil aeration. Of course this is to be expected particularly with corn, since it does after all have ears! We know that music can assist old people to socialize and energize; it can help bring catatonics out of incommunicative isolation, and it can help clarify and structure an emotionally disturbed child's world of feeling.

More dramatic evidence of the hidden influences of music is documented in the following news release from Finland:

> A group of young musicians is being forced to move to a new building because they have upset the cows nearby. Local authorities have ordered the musicians to stop practicing in a building next to a slaughter house because the packing company owners claim the music . . . upsets the cows while they are waiting to die and causes the release of an enzyme in their bodies that makes the meat taste foul. (UPI, 1981)

Unfortunately we do not know what the outcome might have been had the young musicians been asked to play another style of music. Perhaps the flavor of the meat would have improved! In any event, there is an increasing number of indications to support the view that music does indeed have great power to influence behavior, whether it be animal, vegetable, or human.

How many different functions does music serve in your community? Which functions appear to be most successful from your viewpoint? Why?

One might assume that with an increasing abundance of musical styles and functions the general level of human musicality would also be increasing, but the answer to this question hinges on what is meant by the term musicality.

Many tests have been devised to determine individual musical aptitude, or talent as it is sometimes called. Test items usually include pitch, loudness, and timbre discriminations, rhythmic pattern differentiation, and musical memory. While it is true that these attributes are fundamental to musical production and perception, many people believe the nature of musicality is more complex than these isolated abilities.

Outstanding music psychologists like Carl Seashore and James Mursell argued about atomistic and holistic theories of musicality. Mursell (1937) recognized the significance of imagination and thinking and feeling processes in music but was unable to devise valid and reliable methods for determining the precise nature or degree of their involvement.

The Dutch psychologist Geza Revesz (1953) had this to say about the musical person:

> If we would characterize the musical person especially with reference to his sensitivity to artistic quality and his capacity for an aesthetic evaluation of musical works as well as of their artistic performance, then we might add the following: The musical person possesses a deep understanding of musical forms and the structure or movement plan of the work. He has a finely developed sense of style and of the strict organization of musical processes of thought. He is able to follow the composer's intentions, even at times to anticipate them. It is also characteristic of the musical person to sink himself into the mood of the music and achieve a relation to it that has an effect on his whole spiritual being. He experiences the art work so inwardly and so profoundly that he feels as though he were creating it. This "creative" act is peculiar to the musical person not only during the mere aesthetic assimilation, but also in the interpretation of musical works. The possession of these qualities expresses itself in the ability to judge and evaluate the artistic quality of musical works. Musicality—this inborn property that requires (and is also capable of) development—irradiates the whole individual and accordingly forms a characteristic trait of the personality as a whole. (p. 133)

It seems reasonable to argue that a musical person is one who most accurately characterizes the qualities of musicality. It is also reasonable to argue that with the increasing amount of evidence supporting music's many functions, musicality is in fact a multifaceted and complex attribute, probably just as varied and complex as music itself.

> Develop a brief statement describing the most musical person you have ever known. Which of his or her musical traits do you most admire?

It is appropriate therefore that our consideration of the nature of music not be isolated from the nature of musicality because they are obviously intimately connected, particularly as concerns education. If we imagine a musical continuum with very simple tunes or rhythmic patterns at one end, and highly complex instrumental, choral, or electronic structures at the other, then we can also imagine a continuum of musicality where experiencing musical phenomena may vary from very simple aural recognition to a profound involvement of the whole person. It is in these terms that we need to consider the nature of music, moving from recognition of essentially basic physical characteristics of sound, to the synthesis of all sense and thought processes.

DESCRIBING MUSIC: PHYSICAL PROPERTIES

When we think of the physical properties of music, we are primarily concerned with how sounds are produced, that is, with their acoustical characteristics. For example, we are concerned with vibrations that cause sound waves to be projected on to the tympanic membrane or ear drum. We are concerned with the amplitude or intensity of the vibrations, that relates to the distance the vibrating body deviates from its point of rest, and that influences our perceptions of loudness. We are also concerned about the duration of sounds and whether they vary in intensity throughout their duration. Plucked sounds and struck sounds have limited duration potential when compared with blown or bowed or electronically produced sounds. Another concern related to physical production is the frequency of vibration. This relates to the pitch of a tone, so the greater the vibration frequency, the higher the tone in the pitch scale. Our common range of basic pitches employed in music varies from approximately twenty vibrations per second at the lower level to over four thousand vibrations per second at the upper level. However, electronic music sources can easily exceed this higher level, and our general hearing potential extends on up toward and at times beyond 20,000 vibrations per second.

When notes of the same pitch are played on different types of instruments the physical property of wave form is demonstrated. All but the most simple "pure" tones consist of a variety of differing partials. The wave formation influences the quality, tone "color" or timbre of the tone that is heard. Tones with a great many higher partials (harmonics or overtones) present may result in what is frequently termed a rather brilliant or "bright" quality; in contrast, tones with more and stronger lower than upper partials may create the impression of a more sonorous or "dark" quality.

Now that we have sound amplifiers of enormous capacity, we are becoming more aware of the scale of sound intensity that often is measured and described in terms of decibels. Our threshold of hearing is between zero and ten decibels and may be characterized by the gentle rustle of leaves. A nearby jet aircraft may produce up to 120 decibels while amplification at some rock concerts may exceed that level. When sounds approach this high level, acousticians talk about the threshold of feeling or pain, and it is generally recognized that the sensitive components of the ear can be damaged if the intensity level is too great, or even if it is more moderate but experienced for too long. Many persons, musicians as well as others, have suffered serious loss of their hearing ability as a result of excessive exposure to high intensity levels of sound, musical or otherwise.

To be aware of the physical properties of sound in a musical event is somewhat akin to being aware of the calorie count or protein levels in an evening meal. We do not normally wish to analyze or document either experience in great detail, but there are occasions when it is highly desirable to know how musical sounds as well as how foods are constituted. For example, fine tuning of instruments is dependent on some knowledge of vibration, wave formation, and the nature of the overtone series. Similarly, without a knowledge of timbre or tone quality and of how it may be modified in solo or ensemble performance, a teacher, conductor, or composer is severely limited. At present there is a need to know more about decibel or intensity levels and how they affect human hearing and behavior. Acoustical engineers, psychologists, biologists, neurologists, and musicians need to be aware of one another's work and to work together so as to gain deeper insights into some of the areas discussed in this section, particularly the effects of certain kinds of sounds on animal, vegetable, and especially human behaviors.

Few people limit their musical experiences to analyzing the physical properties of sound. Indeed, recent research reinforces the idea that there are significant differences between experiencing sound as sound and sound as music.

Can you recall experiences when you listened to music as sound or sound as music? Do you find it difficult to distinguish between the two? Why?

Jane Siegel (1981) says, "It appears therefore, that listening acoustically is incompatible with listening musically, and that the ability to discriminate fine acoustic variations may actually be detrimental to the enjoyment of music" (p. 215). Siegel's research reinforces Seashore's (1939) conclusions that musical perception involves a degree of illusion rather than "an accurate translation of acoustic reality" (p. 214). Clearly this belief has significant implications for our considerations about the nature of music and particularly the ways in which we experience music; but before we return to the experiencing of music, let us consider two further categories relating to musical properties: formal (including elemental) properties, and aesthetic properties.

DESCRIBING MUSIC: FORMAL PROPERTIES

When we think of musical elements and the formal properties of music, we are thinking less about the physical characteristics of the sounds and more about how the sounds are combined to form music. There is generally no agreed formula for listing all of the formal properties because they are constantly evolving in terms of the art of music. However, *Comprehensive Musicianship: An Anthology of Evolving Thought* from the *Music Educators National Conference* (1971) suggested one model we can consider here. The authors believe that:

A. Music consists of Sound, divisible into
   1. Pitch
       a. horizontal ("melody")
       b. vertical ("harmony")
   2. Duration (rhythm)
   3. Quality
       a. timbre
       b. dynamics
       c. texture
B. These sound elements are used to articulate shape, or *form* (including the possibility of lack of established form).
C. Every musical work must be viewed in its *context*, including stylistic, historical, cultural, and other considerations. (p. 100)

The Hawaii Music Curriculum Project (Thomson, 1974), a curriculum project based on comprehensive musicianship principles, produced a more elaborate model. It developed a taxonomy of concepts, subconcepts and gross associative concepts in which the following seven concepts were considered to be basic to all levels of study: tone, rhythm, melody, harmony, texture, tonality, and form. Within each of these concepts a number of subconcepts were designated. In rhythm, for example, we find the subconcepts of pulse, tempo, rhythmic pattern, meter, accent, duration, simple meter, ritardando, accelerando, compound meter, syncopation, thesis, anacrusis, agogic stress, augmentation, diminution, division of the beat, melodic rhythm, hemiola, composite meter, metric subdivisions, tempo rubato, rhythmic modes, nonmetric proportionate notation (time-space), alla breve, rock accompaniment figures, polymeter, polyrhythm, multimeter, rhythmic motif, elastic or breath rhythm, and colotomic structure.

It will be noted that these subconcepts are arranged in sequence moving from a simple to a more complex order. The same is true for other subconcepts grouped under a major concept. (See figure 1). The gross associative concepts were intended to involve aesthetic response, social function, and historical succession, "and are regarded

Figure 1 Taxonomy of Musical Concepts Arranged by Zones of Instruction

Zone 1 (K–1)

Tone:	pitch, loudness, duration, timbre
Rhythm:	pulse, tempo, rhythmic patterns, meter, accent, duration
Melody:	contour, chant, phrase, speech-song, theme, call-response
Harmony:	simultaneous tones, chord
Texture:	unison, accompaniment
Tonality:	tonic, scale
Form:	phrase, repetition, contrast, introduction, section, recurrence, interlude, coda, variation

Zone II (2–3)

Tone:	definite-indefinite pitch, vibration
Rhythm:	simple meter, ritardando, accelerando, compound meter
Melody:	period, section, cadence, legato, staccato, conjunct, disjunct
Harmony:	chord progression, major-minor, tonic chord
Texture:	simultaneous tones, pedal point (drone)
Tonality:	pentatonic, diatonic, mode
Form:	period, cadence, binary, canon, ternary

Zone III (4–6)

Tone:	instrumentation, vibrato, harmonic series
Rhythm:	syncopation, thesis, anacrusis, agogic stress, augmentation, diminution, division of the beat, melodic rhythm, hemiola, composite meter
Melody:	articulation, interval, diatonic, chromatic, motive, sequence, tonality frame, range, arpeggio, melisma, text setting, glissando, microtone, portamento, chant (Oli), chant (Mele Hula)
Harmony:	tertial harmony, dissonance, consonance, triad, inversion, quartal harmony

Figure 1 *(Continued)*

Texture: monophony, homophony, hocket, imitation, ostinato, fugue, counter-melody, round, band of sound, linear, heterophony

Tonality: key, dominant, cadence, parallel minor, relative minor, natural minor, harmonic minor, modulation, mixolydian mode, Phrygian mode, Aeolian mode, Gagaku mode, 3-tone scale, 4-tone scale, whole tone scale, gamelan anklung scale

Form: theme, antiphony, texture (as determinant of form), rondo, verse, interlude, overture, program music, absolute music, development, sonata-allegro, instrumentation (as determinant of form), strophic, passacaglia, 12 bar blues, aleatory, improvisation, tape processes

Zone IV (7–8)

Tone: frequency, intensity, audible spectrum, dynamics, tone quality, orchestration, special effects (tremolo, indefinite pitch, trill, flutter), silence

Rhythm: metric subdivisions, tempo rubato, rhythmic modes, nonmetric proportionate notation (time-space), alla breve (cut time), rock accompaniment figures

Melody: transposition, phrase structure, bass line, texture as melody, graphic notation

Harmony: parallelism, root, harmonic sequence, nonchord tones, cadence, harmonic rhythm, cluster

Texture: counterpoint, spacing, antiphony

Tonality: mutation, modulation, circle of fifths, atonality, transposition

Form: row-set, sonata form, alea, galliard, villanella

Zone V (9–12)

Tone: wave form, temperament (tuning), formant, decibel scale of intensity, orchestration (solo, tutti, doubling), orchestration (instrument roles), viol tuning, harmonic, Klangfarbenmelodie, overtone series

Rhythm: polymeter, polyrhythm, multimeter, rhythmic motif, elastic or breath rhythm, colotomic structure (Katari and Mororai patterns)

Melody: permutation, "basic melody," step progression, ornamentation, phrase structure (symmetrical, asymmetrical), Gregorian chant, double (variation), dynamic contour, metric stress, thematic group, basic set, inversion, retrograde, retrograde inversion, transposition in performance, transposition by interval and scale

Harmony: nontertial harmony, serial organization, harmonic rhythm, parallelism, voice-leading, resolution, spacing, harmonic density, harmonic sonance, secondary dominant

Texture: pointillism, monody, inversion, number of parts, doubling, prominence of parts, descant, spacing, aleatoric

Tonality: serialism, pandiatonic, polytonality, bitonal, parallel keys, mode (finalis), dodecaphony

Form: traditional form types, ordo-isorhythm, relation to style, electronic procedures, motet, movements, intrada, pavan, galliard, madrigal, Jo-ha-kyu, Netori, Tomede, chanson, concerto grosso, concertato, point of imitation, extension, song form, melodic cantus firmus

Note: Reprinted, with permission of the publisher, from William Thompson, *The Hawaii Music Curriculum Report: The Project Design* (Honolulu: College of Education, University of Hawaii, 1969), p. 12.

as an essential residue that must be nourished in any learning process when the main thrust is directed on the substantive elements of the discipline" (Thomson, 1974, pp. 8–9).

The principal achievement of this project probably is the emphasis it brings to elements and forms of music. Students who study the K-12 curriculum materials are bound to increase their perception of what music is made of and how it is put together. Certainly the Hawaii Music Curriculum Project represents a most carefully structured and detailed attempt to render the elements and forms of music into a sequentially ordered curriculum.

Since the mid 1960s there has been an increasing emphasis on music's formal properties. This has been evident in commercial as well as locally developed curricular materials. Students of music at all levels have been required to participate in musical experiences in ways that increase their understanding of musical elements and forms and that consequently broaden their musical vocabularies and increase their perception of musical events as they unfold.

Sometimes the elements and forms of music have been presented or studied in an overly analytic and simplistic fashion without taking into account the relationships that are generated between the elements and within the forms, relationships that are largely responsible for any resulting aesthetic properties. The process can be like a lesson in anatomy where simply labeling parts of the body will not necessarily increase insight into the miracle of life. Just as humans are more than a collection of bones, muscles, and nerves, so music is more than a collection of rhythms, melodies, and harmonies. It is for this reason that we continue to see an increasing emphasis on the aesthetic properties of music.

DESCRIBING MUSIC: AESTHETIC PROPERTIES

Aesthetic properties can be defined as the comprehensive shapes and patterns of music that emerge from the relationships of the elements and forms. The patterns may be simple or complex, they may possess qualities of predictability as well as unpredictability; sometimes they are easily recognized and sometimes they are extraordinarily elusive or just vaguely suggested. Sometimes they demonstrate qualities of growth and high levels of development, while on other occasions aesthetic properties are dominated by simple repetition or simple contrast.

The elemental and formal properties of music tend to be perceived in isolation from one another. For example, we hear a particular tune or a particular chord progression; our ear distinguishes a rhythmic motif or we notice a gradual crescendo or a unique timbre.

These are essentially unrelated stimuli but when linkage begins to develop in our awareness and the spatial and temporal phenomena of music begin to coalesce, then we begin to perceive larger shapes and patterns that constitute aesthetic properties.

Instead of simply hearing a tune, we hear a musical phrase that has its own contour, its own sense of direction, of growth perhaps that is reinforced by compatible underlying harmonic progressions; furthermore it possesses characteristic qualities, perhaps intervals, pitch frequencies, or qualities of articulation, that connect or relate it to what precedes and to what follows. In this sense the aesthetic properties of a composition are not laid out in successive order like so many groceries in a supermarket. Aesthetic properties are implicit within a composition but they have to be considered and drawn together by the performer and the listener. Of course this takes time. A first hearing of a work may reveal an abundance of elements and forms, but few aesthetic properties. Nevertheless, with repeated hearings and a willingness to explore the work, aesthetic properties may begin to emerge.

The process of experiencing music aesthetically is rather like acquiring a new friend. At first we may be attracted to a person by his or her appearance, or by a response to a question, or by what someone else has said about the person. In any event, there is an initial point of contact and the interest is caught and the relationship begins to develop as more is known on either side. The same is true when we begin to rehearse a new composition. It may be a short piano piece or a very complex and demanding choral or orchestral work. At first we are absorbed with the particulars: the fingerings or bowings, the articulations, melodic and rhythmic accuracy and so on. In a word we are absorbed with the elements. Only gradually as our competence and confidence develops can we begin to do justice to the aesthetic properties. This is when we begin to grasp larger units and to make decisions about such things as points of climax, voicing of parts, importance of inner melodies, dynamic structures, and rhythmic flow. Then each musical event bears a convincing relationship to its temporal and tonal surroundings and the total structure stands revealed. The aesthetic properties then assume primary importance and it is probable or at least possible that an aesthetic experience will follow.

Great works of art tend to be characterized by a vast number of aesthetic properties. That is, they carry within them a seemingly infinite number of inner relationships. The possibilities for exploration, linkage, and penetrating insights are tremendous. Undistinguished works of art seem just the reverse; they tend to be quite predictable, generating instant recognition and reaction, and often fostering somewhat superficial fantasy rather than enduring exploration and education. Harry Broudy (1978) offers some interesting observations along these lines:

> Serious art does in a refined and highly concentrated way what popular art does without conscious tuition. But it explores possibilities of feeling that extend far beyond the routinized experiences of everyday life. Popular art (popular music, the soap operas) portrays the feelings large numbers now share: serious art creates images of feeling that we may have not yet brought to consciousness, sometimes by making the strange familiar; sometimes by making the familiar strange. (p. 9)

Of course, this does not rule out the possibility of popular forms achieving some attributes of "serious" art or of serious art becoming "popular," both of which happen at times; and, it should be recognized that either type or any in between may be "good" in the general functional sense if it is used effectively to fulfill legitimate human needs.

Which have you found more useful in your life thus far, "popular" or "serious" art forms? Which do you believe to have the greater use potential? Aristotle defined art as human intelligence playing over the natural scene, ingeniously manipulating natural resources toward the fulfillment of human purposes (Butcher, 1951). How does such a functional definition compare with your definition of art and music?

Some writers attribute emotional and moral qualities to aesthetic properties. For example, they claim that honesty, integrity, purity, or sincerity are hallmarks of aesthetic excellence. Such is not the view taken here. Rather, we believe it is important to distinguish between the nature of a work, that is, how it can be described, and the kinds of human behaviors evoked or stimulated by that work. If we do this, then we will avoid the arguments that inevitably arise when we try to ascribe specific emotional or moral characteristics to a particular composition. Of course no one, and least of all teachers, would wish to deny the extraordinary capacity music has for illuminating our own inner lives, our unique personal nature, our own values. For that reason we need to explore how this can best be accomplished.

If we were to cease considering the nature of music at this point we would not know how musical properties can be experienced. It is the musical experience that is of primary concern here because unless music is experienced, we can hardly hope for it to be educational. To describe the properties of a phenomenon, whether they be music, a flower, or another human being, is one thing, but to experience that phenomenon is something else. So, let us consider the process involved when we internalize music.

You may have difficulty in attempting to distinguish between describing properties and experiencing those properties. It may help to think of other forms of human experience in which the properties can be considered separately from the ways in which we experience them. For example, what about a plane and a plane ride; or a meal viewed on the table and a meal consumed; or a description of a particular game and actually playing that game. Discuss these distinctions in class and compare them with describing music and experiencing music.

EXPERIENCING MUSIC—AS IMAGERY

A vitally important part of the music experience is what we ourselves bring to music. In general terms the psychologist Jane Siegel (1981) writes: "Human perception is as much determined by the perceiver, his experience and his expectations, as it is by the stimulus" (p. 96). In artistic terms Jacob Bronowski (1978) writes: "The work of art is essentially an unfinished statement. It presents you with this so you will make your own generalization from it" (p. 126). He also says that "the work of art does not exist for you unless you also recreate it" (p. 143). And Maxine Greene (1971) writes that "an aesthetic object depends upon a living subject for its coming into being" (p. 24).

These views coincide with ours in stressing the fundamental importance of the human component in the musical experience. The question then arises as to the nature of that component. What can or should we contribute to a musical event so that the experience achieves its fullest potential? Obviously perception of the physical, elemental, formal, and aesthetic properties has to be the foundation of the musical experience. The process of listening, hearing, and identifying these properties is the launching pad, so to speak. But the perception of these properties has to relate to our own experiential world if the music is to be humanly significant. One way of achieving this is through our capacity to generate imagery. This is a natural creative process which we enjoy from early childhood when we learn by projecting ourselves into all kinds of imaginary worlds.

Some people argue that television inhibits or destroys a child's capacity to imagine because that medium provides a nearly total experience, drawing the child into its web and drowning the individual senses and creative potential as it does so. On the other hand, music is basically an aural stimulus that, when internalized, opens all kinds of personal palaces and dungeons, places to hide, places to explore and live in. Adults formalize their images in operas and plays but the process is similar. Sometimes imagery is built into a composition as in Saint-Saëns's *Carnival of the Animals* or Prokofiev's *Peter and the Wolf*.

The same kind of thing happens in Grofé's *Grand Canyon Suite*, or Copland's *Appalachian Spring*, Beethoven's *Pastoral Symphony*, Tchaikovsky's *Pathétique Symphony*, Vivaldi's *The Seasons*—the list of musical compositions with fairly explicit imagery is long and distinguished. Imagery may be related to religious events as in settings of the Mass, or to patriotic events as in marches or overtures like Tchaikovsky's *1812*. Of course there are enormous quantities of music that have been composed without any deliberate suggestion of accompanying imagery, but that does not prevent performers or listeners from providing images of their own devising if they so desire. Some people find color imagery appropriate for their listening habits, while others imagine landscapes or seascapes or even moonscapes! Still others visualize abstract shapes and patterns as they relate to the flowing densities and interweaving threads.

The examples of pictorial imagery given here represent some of the more obvious ways in which people can flesh out the tonal phenomena in terms of their own existences. Many music teachers might argue that this kind of imagery does little to assist musical perception and they may be right. On the other hand, if the musical experience becomes more vital and more personal as a result of such imagery, then it is also likely to become more enjoyable. Certainly a musical experience is of doubtful value if it is not appreciated and so we should not belittle the importance of imagery in music education or in general education. As Bronowski (1978) says: "Imagination simply means the human habit of making images inside one's head. And the ability to make these personal images is the giant step in the evolution of man and in the growth of every child" (p. 11).

When we ask a child if a short musical event reminds him of something, we are encouraging imaginative growth. Similarly, if we ask a child to create a short musical event about a particular experience or place, or animal, or person, we are fostering an attitude toward his or her imaginative life that recognizes and encourages individuality and self-esteem.

This kind of image making represents the natural beginnings of linkage between tonal and human phenomena; it provides a base on which to build more sophisticated and profound relationships as we grow. Broudy (1978) speaks of imagery in this sense as well as in the more general sense when he argues that aesthetic experience is a basic necessity. He points out that, while science can tell us *why* we have feelings, only images supplied by art can tell us *what* they mean. "Aesthetic experience is basic because it is a primary form of experience on which all cognition, judgment, and action depend. It is the fundamental and distinctive power of image making by the imagination" upon which all scientific thinking must be based. Broudy concludes that aesthetic imagery provides the raw material for concepts and ideas, for creativity, for "a world of possibility" (p. 8).

EXPERIENCING MUSIC—METAPHORICALLY

A metaphor involves a degree of abstraction that goes beyond imagery. Metaphoric experience is more removed from actual places and things or people; it is more inward than the image and has to do primarily with qualities of feeling and qualities of movement that are evoked by tonal phenomena. The term "feeling moved" sums up this kind of metaphoric experience because it draws together two of our most basic human conditions, namely, feeling and movement.

Humans move through time and space, we exist in time and space, and we react with feeling to tonal and other relationships that evolve in time and space. For some, the quality of movement and feeling may be severely limited; our range of movement experience may be narrow due to geographic conditions, economic limitations, or other factors. Similarly, our range of feeling experience may be shallow, poorly defined, or constricted. Others may experience far-ranging and variable movement, and intense depths of feeling. The feeling of being moved varies from quite simple conditions to the most profoundly complex states.

The vocabulary for describing and exploring this kind of metaphoric experience is somewhat limited and open to criticism. Some of this criticism can be traced to the habit of associating the vocabulary with the tonal phenomena, rather than with the way those phenomena are experienced. As we have seen, the vocabulary we employ to describe tonal phenomena, whether it be physical, elemental, formal, or aesthetic, is rather precise. It is a professional vocabulary used by ever-increasing numbers of discriminating performers and listeners. On the other hand, an experiential vocabulary does not have this kind of precision because it is more personal and intimate, more vivid and colorful, and is obviously derived from the ways in which we each experience tonal phenomena as individuals.

The development of linguistic skills in relation to any art form is difficult but nevertheless vitally important. Psychologists and researchers are beginning to devote much more attention to this matter. For example, Roger Brown (1981) says:

> Emotional language comes nearer than other language to conveying the musical experience. Perhaps technical musical language is more precise, but it is only known to a relatively small community. There must be some affinity linking emotional and musical experience that causes nonmusicians, at least, to use the former as metaphor for the latter. It did not arise from any conspiracy of the enemies of music, if such there be.

Eventually, I would guess, we shall find a new sort of terminology . . . far more precise than is now offered by English, French, German, or Italian. (p. 242)

If we consider the possibilities of a metaphoric vocabulary derived from the condition of feeling moved, we have the possibility on the one hand of words that clearly relate either to feeling or to movement, while on the other hand we have words that relate to both feeling and movement. For example, fast and slow are obviously qualities of movement just as happy and sad are qualities of feeling, but words such as vitality, exhilaration, turbulent, or triumphant, connote qualities of feeling and movement that may be experienced simultaneously.

Share with the class a short musical excerpt that has great meaning for you and be prepared to explain why.

These words evoking qualities of movement and feeling at the same time would seem to replicate most honestly the condition of feeling moved. So let us consider this vocabulary further and explore some of its implications. We are saying in effect that this kind of metaphoric experience derived from tonal phenomena is not just simple feeling or simple movement. The experience is more complex and contains qualities of feeling and movement as the sounds interact in time and space.

Just as we found it important to develop linkage in developing perception of physical, formal, and aesthetic properties, so it is important to seek linkage in the experiential domain. A person whose experience of music is limited to imagery (in the narrow sense) is comparable with one whose perception of music is limited to the physical properties of sounds or to the basic formal elements of rhythm, tone, or melody. Our concern, therefore, is to broaden the experience of music just as we attempt to broaden the range of musical perception. Imagery may be a valid point of entry for many people to experience music, but, if the process stops there, human potential as well as musical potential remains underdeveloped.

Similarly, if musical experience is limited to simple feelingful states such as happy, sad, or angry, or simple qualities of movement such as fast and slow, or skipping and jumping, then the experience is clearly undernourished. It is not surprising that many music educators feel upset or insulted when they hear of teachers who ask their students naive questions such as, "Is the music happy or sad?" Clearly, this approach does not do justice to how music is or may be experienced even at preschool levels. The question implies that music can and should be reduced to a series of feelings strung out like a soap opera that titillates our dulled senses.

To experience music in a metaphoric way is to be aware of a unique blend of feeling and movement that is generated as the sounds interact in space and time. A music critic sometimes employs a phrase that combines these two qualities, allowing the reader or the listener to gain a clearer perspective on a particular experience. We may read that the music evoked a "joyous outburst" or a "restless impulse," or perhaps "the melodies were gently persuasive" but they contrasted with occasional "irregular explosive accents." There may be "strong vital statements" or "fragile and tentative moments," periods of "luster and vibrance" or "outpourings of restless energy." These are phrases that attempt to do justice to some of the complexities involved in experiencing music metaphorically. They do not describe the sound phenomena as such, but, rather, how those phenomena might be experienced by at least one listener or performer.

There are undoubtedly many words that could contribute to a metaphoric vocabulary describing the condition of feeling moved. Among them might be: calm, confused, eager, energetic, exhausted, frantic, frightened, proud, relaxed, tenuous, violent, vital, mechanical, dramatic. These are words that convey for most people a sense of feeling as well as movement. Sometimes it may be more effective or more accurate to employ combinations of words such as: intimate tenuous sounds, angular melodic outcries, relentless rhythmic drive, penetrating intensities, terse fragmented statements, violent twisting rhythmic forces, clear economic elegance, or bleak dissonance.

If we are genuinely concerned with developing the quality of the musical experience we *need* to explore the language connection. Only then can we hope to identify and develop those forces that contribute to our feeling moved when we experience music. Language is not the same experience, the words are not the same feelings; but language is the essential tool that allows us to conceptualize and think about, to analyze and teach about these vital musical matters that ultimately can take us beyond words.

In Robert Burns's poem "The Rose and The Thorn," the lover says, "You stole the rose and left the thorn." Broudy (1978, p. 8) wonders about the thousands of lines of psychological analysis it would take to clarify the feeling expressed in this metaphor, and, we would add, in a well-formed musical metaphor. Still, we must build on more basic communications such as prosaic words and expressive gestures in our teaching so that musical meanings beyond the verbal and visual may be experienced more readily and effectively. We should note that not many musicians have ever been justly accused of being highly effective from the verbal standpoint. Leonard Bernstein is one of the notable contemporary exceptions. It is essential that music *teachers* be verbally effective.

Listen to a musical excerpt in class and compile some short statements that attempt to capture metaphoric musical experience.
Share your statements and discuss them in terms of the variety
and vividness of the experiences.

EXPERIENCING MUSIC—AS ANALOGY

One more area of musical experience needs to be considered here,
as a further step in abstraction beyond simple imagery and metaphor.
It also represents a further step in the linkage process between musical
phenomena and human experience.

When we experience music as a life analog, we move beyond the
fragmentary nature of imagery and the personal experiences of feeling moved. Instead, we begin to recognize within the musical experience an identity with life itself; not just feeling and movement per
se, but the whole dynamics of living. We recognize ongoing cycles of
musical events that replicate the cycles of life events with an extraordinary degree of accuracy and truth.

To experience music in terms of a living analog is to identify
oneself with the tonal events as they unfold, to assume a state of being
that is both in the music and outside oneself. It is perhaps most closely
akin to a journey in which our means of transportation takes us from
point A to point B with all kinds of expected and unexpected happenings en route. Directions change, speeds vary, energies and ten-
sions build and wane; we gravitate here, we deviate there; we anticipate
and then we are reassured, or surprised; we are confident and stable,
but at times also uncertain, insecure, and doubtful; perspectives shift,
momentums change, suggestions become realities, distortions focus
into truths, and insights are confirmed.

Our experiential vocabulary has shifted from one that centers on
affective states to one that captures a fluid living process. To experience this relationship between music and life is to enjoy one of the
most rewarding experiences music has to offer. Our day-to-day life
experiences frequently are either too crisis laden or too common,
inconclusive, interrupted, unfulfilled, or amorphous to provide significant meaning and joy. But music can help us to clarify our thoughts
and feelings: By experiencing its meaningful structures, we can gain
meaningful insights into our lives, into ourselves. It is here that we
are reassured about some of the most basic human qualities and values
to which we aspire, that are revealed within the musical experience.
If the musical experience is of this order, we are revived and refreshed
and there is a renewed confidence in the human condition.

A life-analog vocabulary can include words such as anticipation,
cohesion, complexity, consistency, continuity, convergence, decay, de-

ception, deviation, direction, distortion, expectation, gravitation, growth, intensity, order, organization, perspective, probability, resistance, resolution, stability, tendency, and tension. These words are obviously not as important as the processes they stand for, but, without the words, there is the danger that we remain ignorant of the processes, or only vaguely aware of their significance. Thus we emphasize the necessity of the language tool that seems to be a prime lack in the preparation of many music educators.

Leonard Meyer (1956) writes:

> The grammatical aspect of music varies from culture to culture and from style to style within a culture. What remains constant are not scales, modes, harmonic progressions or formal procedures, but the psychology of human mental processes—the way in which the mind, operating within the context of a culturally established grammar, selects and organizes and evaluates the musical materials presented to it. For instance, the desire of the human mind for completeness and stability is a psychological constant. (p. 274)

Similarly, we seek novelty, we develop expectations and tendencies, we look for a sense of direction, of order, of development, and, as we do so, we experience growth, gravitation, tension, and resolution. These are life processes of the most fundamental kind and if we do not possess some insight into the way they function naturally in our day-to-day lives, how they can be dealt with and channeled to our human benefit, we are likely to experience enormous frustration and wasted human potential.

Because music exists in time and space and is created by humans existing in time and space, it provides an analog of these life processes. Through music we are able to gain new insights into ourselves, new perspectives that are seemingly impossible when we are embedded in moment-to-moment and day-to-day activities. Because the nature of mankind tends to be man's greatest interest and concern, because we are our own greatest puzzle, and because music has the capacity to function as a powerful tool for self-revelation and understanding, we find it valuable, need-fulfilling, and thus satisfying and enjoyable. Effective education helps us learn to value the kinds of musical experiences that take us through an extraordinarily rich maze of structural intensities; we come to value the personal and human insights, the logic, the resolution, and the confidence that these musical experiences provide.

Figure 2 (Tait, 1980, p. 51) represents a summation of the preceding discussions about the properties of music and how music may be experienced. This figure illustrates the kinds of personal-musical

Figure 2 The Nature of Musical Experience as a Synthesis of Tonal and Human Phenomena

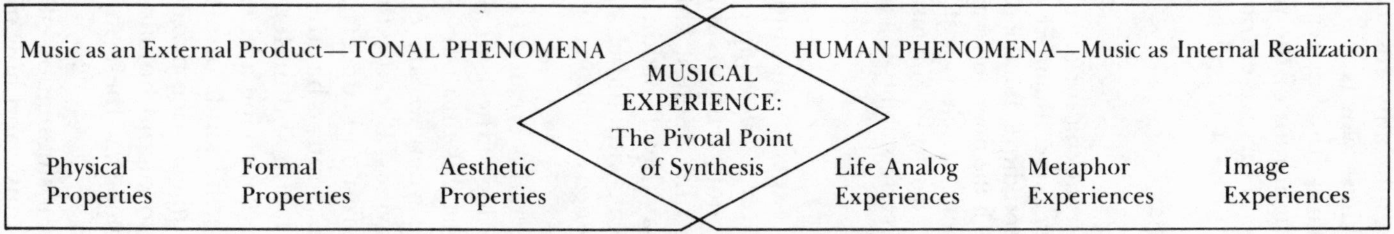

Music as an External Product—TONAL PHENOMENA			MUSICAL EXPERIENCE: The Pivotal Point of Synthesis	HUMAN PHENOMENA—Music as Internal Realization		
Physical Properties	Formal Properties	Aesthetic Properties		Life Analog Experiences	Metaphor Experiences	Image Experiences

EXAMPLES

Physical Properties	Formal Properties	Aesthetic Properties	Life Analog Experiences	Metaphor Experiences	Image Experiences
Vibration	Tone	Line	Energy	Angry	Colorful
Envelope	Melody	Shape	Growth	Gentle	Angular
Intensity	Rhythm	Space	Stability	Peaceful	Cavernous
Duration	Harmony	Style	Deviation	Floating	Pastoral
Wave Form	Sonata	Design	Gravitation	Bouncing	Religious
Production	Rondo	Pattern	Complexity	Charging	Patriotic

Note: Adapted from Malcolm Tait, "Self in Sound," *Music Educators Journal,* November 1980, p. 51. Used by permission of the publisher.

interactions that develop with an awareness of music and an involvement with it.

At one extreme our awareness may be limited to the perception of physical or formal properties, and, based on that perception, there may be the beginnings of image or metaphoric experience. Alternatively, a perception of aesthetic properties may be accompanied by linkage to image, metaphor, and life analog experiences. Of course these linkages are not clearly defined steps or stages of musical growth; rather, they are tentative gestures toward internalizing musical phenomena in ways that make music more meaningful and valuable.

As the linkage between musical properties and musical experiences becomes more sophisticated and complex, we move beyond what might be termed musical processing toward a more profoundly satisfying aesthetic experience. The aesthetic properties are then perceived and supported by an awareness of elemental and formal relationships; but, more significantly, these same aesthetic properties are linked to life analogs and metaphors so that they become personally significant and move the listener into the realm of aesthetic experience.

Such linkage between properties and experiences is not automatic; it requires a willingness on the part of musical consumers and producers to commit themselves to the flow of musical events and invest themselves in those events. In this sense an aesthetic experience will not accrue solely from the recognition of aesthetic properties. An aesthetic experience requires a personal identity with aesthetic properties by means of life analogs. Aesthetic experiences are profoundly complex and deeply satisfying occurrences that generally do not come about simply or automatically. They represent the apex of all forms of artistic education, the product of our finest efforts in relating artistic phenomena to human experience.

> Listen to a musical excerpt and make notes in answer to the following questions: What is the music about? What is the music made of? How is the music put together? How is the music produced? How "good" is this music? Compare your notes in class.

THINKING, FEELING, AND SHARING MUSIC

Just as human beings have been described as thinking, feeling, and sharing creatures, music, as a highly significant product of such creatures, must involve thinking, feeling, and sharing behaviors and experiences. You may have noticed that in the "Describing Music" sections of this chapter thinking behaviors tended to be emphasized. And in the "Experiencing Music" sections feeling behaviors tended to be emphasized. Though such emphases seem natural, we cannot be misled into believing that they are totally discrete functions. Certainly the description of musical properties can involve more than thinking, and the experiencing of music can involve more than feeling. We realize that thinking or feeling may be emphasized at various times in our musical behaviors; but the key to quality in musical experience is the balance, the constant interaction, the ongoing interplay of thinking and feeling, the involvement and application of our whole human capacity in our musical behaviors.

Thinking and feeling modes of behavior tend to parallel one another, and generally precede the sharing mode. A thoughtful understanding of musical properties interacting and coordinating with a feelingful awareness of musical experiences can provide a quality of musical behavior worthy of sharing. Appropriate linking of the phenomena and the experiences provides the basis for a depth of sharing that can stimulate and thus illuminate our whole human potential. Figure 3 diagrams this linkage.

Musical properties are "internal" to the music just as musical experiences are "internal" to the producer/consumer; but both are interactive operations. Sharing is their just combination, their blending, and their externalization. If thought-oriented properties are greatly overemphasized, there is danger of sterility; and if feeling-oriented experiences are greatly overemphasized, there is danger of emotional chaos. Neither condition is worthy of our true human potential, our musical potential, nor of sharing.

Think about and discuss other likely results of severe imbalance in human behavior in general, as well as in musical behavior in particular.

Sharing is that external interactive operation in which thoughtful/ feelingful musical experiences are externalized via interactive musical

Figure 3   An Overview of the Relationship Among Musical Properties, Experiences, and Behaviors

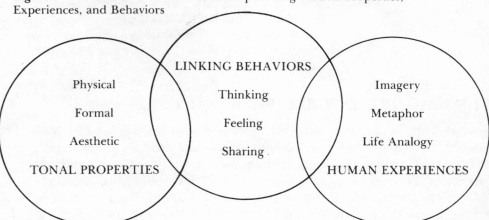

behaviors. Such external interactions involve verbal and/or nonverbal musical behaviors. While language remains a valued tool for sharing everything that can be known and experienced, nonverbal behaviors play a particularly vital role in the sharing of music because of music's nature. Such nonverbal behaviors can be classified under the general headings of musical composition, performance, listening, as well as bodily gesture and facial expression (as employed in conducting, performing, teaching, and learning). Thinking, feeling, and the various aspects of sharing will continue to be illuminated and developed as we move from theoretical to practical levels in this book.

In our first chapter, we introduced our concepts of thinking, feeling, and sharing in rather general terms and without precise definition. As we consider these behaviors in more detail, and particularly as we consider the ways in which they relate to music and the experiencing of music, we need more precise understanding and consistent usage. Therefore we have chosen to define thinking as emphasizing linear, analytic, deductive, logical, more specific processes. Feeling behaviors then emphasize nonlinear, spatial, sensing, imagining, divergent, intuitive, and more general processes. The mind represents the internal meeting ground for thinking and feeling processes, "the human consciousness that originates in the brain and is manifested especially in thought, perception, feeling, will, memory or imagination . . . the totality of conscious and unconscious processes of the brain and central nervous system that directs the mental and physical behavior of a sentient organism" (*The American Heritage Dictionary*). Sharing behaviors are external interactions that result from the internal interactions of the thinking and feeling processes. Sharing behaviors result from the creative and just combination of thinking and feeling and may be verbal as well as nonverbal interactions. Sharing is the outcome of internal interactions. It serves to clarify, communicate, and educate.

> Debate the credibility of the following claims: (a) Because music is essentially a form of communication, all music is for sharing; (b) because it is a sociocultural phenomenon, influenced by and expressive of cultural values, even music which is composed, performed, or heard by a single individual in isolation is an act of sharing with others past, present, or future.

It may be helpful and interesting to look to the history of music in Western civilization to see what types of expressions remain useful, illuminating, enjoyable, and thus shareable today. If we take a general overview, we find some alternating or cycling of classical and romantic emphases, but rarely do we find extreme examples from either type of era in the extant repertoire. The thought-provoking formal properties of symphonies by Haydn, Mozart, and early Beethoven remain appealing, but the overly academic and cognitive puzzles of sound emanating from composers such as Dittersdorf and others of the same era are of interest only to musicologists and a few other specialists, and thus rarely heard. In like manner, we still use and enjoy the expressive and feelingful music of Beethoven, Brahms, Chopin, Wagner, Verdi, and many others (including Bach), but the overly affective, romantic potboilers have gone by the wayside or found a useful existence only as background for comedy, melodrama, or television cartoons.

Which eras or periods of Western history tend to be more classically or formally oriented and which tend to be more romantically or affectively oriented? Are there similar contrasts in non-Western civilizations? What are some of the sociocultural factors that determine or influence the musical mode of expression?

This begs the question of values and endurance: Is it probable that of all the music from the recent history of Western civilization, the music of the three "B's" (Bach, Beethoven, and Brahms) and several notable others remains most viable, used, and presumably valuable because it tends best to balance and integrate the thoughtful and the feelingful aspects of the art and of our humanity? Possibly the balance of thought-provoking properties and feelingful qualities in this music provides for their mutual enhancement in such a way that in-depth awareness of the sounds stimulates a base for higher realms of thought and feeling, leading to a spiral of elevating experience. If so, such music may continue to offer revelations of human potential and the ideal human condition via a quality and depth that remains worthy of sharing through the ages.

To be worthy of sharing, music must be perceived as valuable; and, to be perceived as valuable, it must be meaningful and useful. We have stressed that to be maximally meaningful to man, a thinking, feeling, sharing being, music must emulate these attributes in its properties and potentials and be experienced accordingly. However, we also recognize the fact that maximal potentials and ideals are only rarely achieved. Fortunately, varying qualities and forms of music that hold at least some expressive meaning, even to the inclusion of subconscious influences, may be of significant use and thus of value in the lives of persons. Of course, for the same reasons music may also be abused or unjustly used to influence or control human behavior, and today as never before persons must be educated to this fact as well: Human dignity and freedom can be as readily demeaned as enhanced by the use of music. (See Haack, 1982.)

What are some of the more common, everyday uses that you
make of music in your life? Which help you to be a more effective
person? How? Discuss some ways in which music may be abused,
used illegitimately.

We need to address one final and vitally important question about
music: Why is it valuable? We have already said what may be music's
highest function—the revelation of the nature and potential of people, by people, for people—and we have held these truths to be self-
evident. However, the marvelous thing about the musical medium is
that it is so multifunctional, and thus multivaluable. Though we may
not be as aware of its other functions and value potentials, both we
and our students should be, since these functions and values abound
in our musically saturated world today. We should know the broad
range of potential musical uses and functions to keep from being
abused by them, as well as to use them wisely for our own legitimate
personal and social purposes, for the fulfillment of our own needs
and those of others.

From a considerable body of research, Alan Merriam (1964) con-
cluded in his *Anthropology of Music* that "music is clearly indispensable
to the proper promulgation of the activities that constitute a society;
it is a universal human behavior—without it, it is questionable that
man could truly be called man, with all that implies" (p. 227). In
conjunction with this statement Merriam listed ten functions of music,
though he did not claim them to be necessarily discrete nor all-
inclusive. In describing the functions of music, Merriam elaborated
on: emotional expression; aesthetic enjoyment (note that the aesthetic
is indeed a function, a highly important one, but one of many); entertainment; communication (for many purposes including personal,
commercial, and as propaganda); symbolic representation; the stimulation of physical response; the engendering of conformity to social
norms; validation of social institutions and religious rituals; and contribution to the continuity and stability of culture (chap. 11).

In a similar manner, E. Thayer Gaston (1968), "the father of music
therapy," surveyed a great deal of literature and came to the following
conclusions: All mankind has a need for aesthetic expression and
experience; the cultural matrix determines the mode and meaning
of musical expression; music is communication; music is structured
reality; music and religion are integrally related; music is derived
essentially from the tender emotions and is generally an expression
of good will; music is often shared group activity; and music is a
source of gratification and need fulfillment (chap. 1).

Finally we conclude, with Merriam (1964), that music is important,
useful, and valuable because "there is probably no other human cul-

tural activity which is so all-pervasive and which reaches into, shapes, and often controls [as well as reveals] so much of human behavior" (p. 218). Of course, neither he nor we were the first to think about such things; nor, we would guess, was Aristotle, who felt strongly that music has the power of affecting character, and because it has this power, it is clear that man must be directed to it, and be educated in it (Butcher, 1951).

EXTENSIONS

Statements

1. "Music structures feeling but also impregnates structure with feeling. It is a merging of subjectivity and objectivity." Swanwick, Keith, *A Basis for Music Education* (Windsor, England: NFER-Nelson Publishing Co., 1979), p. 112.
2. "If we take a purely psychological approach, then we will be conscious of everything that goes on within us in our response to, and enjoyment of, musical works, of the direct experience in musical perception. In the phenomenological approach attention is directed primarily upon the work, the structure, the compositional pattern, the architecture, the inner forces manifesting themselves in the art work. Through both avenues we can try to penetrate into the aesthetic sphere." Revesz, G., *Introduction to the Psychology of Music* (London: Longmans, Green, 1953), p. 237.
3. "It is a shocking fact that the nature and value of music are not under-stood by many who teach it. Inevitably, this makes much of music ed-ucation unmusical in nature and in value." Reimer, Bennett, *A Philosophy of Music Education* (Englewood Cliffs, N.J.: Prentice-Hall, 1970), p. 9.
4. "The grammatical aspect of music varies from culture to culture and from style to style within a culture. What remains constant are not scales, modes, harmonic progressions, or formal procedures, but the psychol-ogy of human mental processes—the way in which the mind operating within the context of a culturally established grammar selects and or-ganizes and evaluates the musical materials presented to it. For instance, the desire of the human mind for completeness and stability is a psy-chological constant." Meyer, Leonard B., "Universalism and Relativism in the Study of Ethnic Music," in *Readings in Ethnomusicology*, ed. David P. McAllester (New York: Johnson Reprint Corp., 1971), p. 274.
5. "Concern for the sound as an end in itself, or for the social means to the attainment of that end, are two aspects of musical creativity that cannot be separated, and both seem to be present in many societies. Whether the emphasis is on humanly organized sound or on soundly organized humanity, on a tonal experience related to people or a shared experience related to tones, the function of music is to reinforce, or relate people more closely to, certain experiences which have come to

have meaning in their social life." Blacking, John, *How Musical Is Man?*
(London: Faber and Faber, 1973), p. 99.

Questions and Suggestions

1. To what extent does your choice of a major performing instrument
   (including voice) reflect the nature of your musical aptitude?
2. To what extent does "musicality" determine success in music?
3. Is musicality general or specific? Is it socially determined or genetically
   determined, or both perhaps? How does musicality differ from talent
   or musical aptitude or musical achievement?
4. What are some of the ways in which the psychology of music might
   assist our understanding of musical ability?
5. Does your definition of musical aptitude differ from your concept of a
   musical person? Why?
6. Must a composition communicate in order to be successful?
7. Can music be an introduction to life as well as an escape from life?
8. Some people believe that, musically speaking, we are putting the pack-
   aging ahead of the product in our contemporary society. Do you agree?
   If so, do you see any problems with this?
9. What are some of the values to be gained from the study of non-Western
   musics in the classroom?
10. Develop an experiment that will isolate and illustrate one of the physical
    properties of sound. You may wish to think of a particular age level to
    provide a focus for your demonstration-experiment.
11. Find three differing definitions of the term "aesthetic." Which definition
    is most meaningful to you? Why?
12. Choose a listening example you are unfamiliar with. On your first hear-
    ing analyze the physical properties of the music as carefully and as fully
    as you can. On your second hearing, take particular note of the elemental
    and formal properties of the music. With the third hearing, listen in-
    tently for aesthetic properties. Then prepare a brief statement about
    each process.
13. What are some of your favorite works with explicit imagery? Would
    you enjoy them as much if you were unfamiliar with the program or
    text?
14. What are some of your favorite works without explicit imagery? Would
    you enjoy them as much if some imagery were suggested? Suppose you
    might wish to associate some kind of imagery with one of those com-
    positions. What would you choose and why?
15. How many words can you think of that combine qualities of movement
    and qualities of feeling? Prepare a list for class sharing and try to relate
    some of the words to some selected listening examples which you per-
    sonally think are appropriate to them. Analyze your examples (in musical
    terms), as concerns their relationships to the appropriate words.
16. Can the same performance be musically rewarding for the performer
    and unrewarding for the audience, or vice versa? Why or why not?
17. Discuss the implications of musical meaning as distinct from musical
    content. To what extent may music educators be placing too great an

emphasis on the content of music rather than on the meanings inherent in the musical experience? What would be some of the educational implications if the process were to be reversed?

18. Is the dichotomy of teaching for perception or teaching for response more apparent than real? What are the psychological and musical assumptions that must be made before the problem can be resolved?

19. Discuss the assertion that "the musical ear is less important than the musical imagination." Explore the implications of this statement for music education.

20. If music could be considered on a continuum from "good" to "bad," what are the factors that might influence such qualitative judgments and what are their implications for music education?

21. What do you imagine when you imagine music? What do you feel when you feel music? What do you think when you think music? What do you experience when you listen to music? What do you experience when you perform music?

22. Music is often considered in terms of rhythm, melody, harmony, tonality, forms, and so forth, but what would be the implications for music education if we started to think of music more frequently in terms of qualities of living such as stability, growth, direction, energy, or subtlety?

REFERENCES AND READINGS

Bronowski, Jacob. *The Visionary Eye*. Cambridge: MIT Press, 1978.

Broudy, Harry. "How Basic Is Aesthetic Education or Is 'Rt the Fourth R?" *Bulletin of the Council for Research in Music Education*, no. 57, Winter 1978, pp. 1–10.

Brown, Roger. "Music and Language." In *Documentary Report of the Ann Arbor Symposium: Applications of Psychology to the Teaching and Learning of Music*. Reston, Va.: Music Educators National Conference, 1981.

Butcher, S. H. *Aristotle's Theory of Poetry and Fine Art*. New York: Dover, 1951.

Copland, Aaron. *Music and Imagination*. New York: Mentor Books, 1952.

Dahlhaus, Carl. *Esthetics of Music*, translated by William Austin. Cambridge: Cambridge University Press, 1982.

Dewey, John. *Art as Experience*. New York: Capricorn Books, 1958.

Epperson, Gordon. *The Musical Symbol*. Ames: Iowa State University Press, 1967.

Farnsworth, Paul R. *The Social Psychology of Music*. Ames: Iowa State University Press, 1969.

Gaston, E. Thayer, ed. *Music in Therapy*. New York: Macmillan, 1968.

Greene, Maxine. "Teaching for Aesthetic Experience." In *Toward an Aesthetic Education*. Reston, Va.: Music Educators National Conference, 1971.

Haack, Paul. "Is Big Brother Watching?" *Music Educators Journal*, May 1982, pp. 25–27.

Hebb, D. O. "The Mind and Its Integration." In *Control of the Mind*, edited by S. M. Farber and R. H. L. Wilson. New York: McGraw-Hill, 1961.

Hughes, C. W. *The Human Side of Music*. New York: Philosophical Library, 1948.

Langer, Susanne K. *Philosophy in a New Key*. New York: Mentor Books, 1961.

Langer, Susanne K. *Feeling and Form*. New York: Scribner's, 1953.

Merriam, Alan P. *The Anthropology of Music*. Chicago: Northwestern University Press, 1964.

Meyer, Leonard B. "Universalism and Relativism in the Study of Ethnic Music." In *Readings in Ethnomusicology*. New York: Johnson Reprint Corporation, 1971.

Meyer, Leonard B. *Emotion and Meaning in Music*. Chicago: University of Chicago Press, 1956.

Mursell, James L. *Psychology of Music*. New York: W. W. Norton, 1937.

Music Educators National Conference (MENC). *Music in World Cultures*. Washington: MENC, 1972.

Music Educators National Conference (MENC). *Comprehensive Musicianship: An Anthology of Evolving Thought*. Washington: MENC, 1971.

Paynter, John, and Aston, Peter. *Sound and Silence*. Cambridge: Cambridge University Press, 1970.

Philipson, Morris, and Gudel, Paul J. *Aesthetics Today*. New York: Meridian Books, New American Library, 1980.

Rader, Melvin, ed. *A Modern Book of Aesthetics*. New York: Holt, Rinehart and Winston, 1965.

Radocy, R. E., and Boyle, J. D. *Psychological Foundations of Musical Behavior*. Springfield, Ill.: Charles C. Thomas, 1979.

Read, Herbert. *The Meaning of Art*. Middlesex, England: Penguin Books, 1949.

Reid, Louis Armand. *Meaning in the Arts*. London: George Allen and Unwin, 1969.

Reimer, Bennett. *A Philosophy of Music Education*. Englewood Cliffs, N. J.: Prentice-Hall, 1970.

Revesz, G. *Introduction to the Psychology of Music*. London: Longmans, Green, 1953.

Roederer, Jaun G. *Introduction to the Physics and Psychophysics of Music*. London: English Universities Press, 1974.

Schwadron, Abraham A. *Aesthetics: Dimensions for Music Education*. Washington: Music Educators National Conference, 1967.

Seashore, Carl E. *Psychology of Music*. New York: McGraw-Hill, 1939.

Sessions, Roger. *The Musical Experience of Composer, Performer, Listener*. Princeton, N.J.: Princeton University Press, 1971.

Siegel, Jane A. "Culturally Defined Learning Experience." In *Documentary Report of the Ann Arbor Symposium*. Reston, Va.: Music Educators National Conference, 1981.

Stravinsky, Igor. *The Poetics of Music*. New York: Vintage Books, 1956.

Tait, Malcolm. "Self in Sound: Properties and Qualities of the Musical Experience." *Music Educators Journal*, November 1980, pp. 50–51.

Thomson, William. *The Hawaii Music Curriculum Project: The Project Design*. Honolulu: University of Hawaii, 1974.

UPI Press Release in *Times–Sun*, Kotka, Finland, November 9, 1981.

3
Education

Underlying Concepts: Education is the linkage between people and their experiences that helps to make those experiences meaningful and valuable.

A primary goal of education in a democracy is the balancing of self and society, of personal development and sharing the fruits of that development. Therefore education must be a process of realizing individual and social potential in a personal yet mutually enhancing manner.

The arts provide insight into cultural, historical, and individual identities and provide lifelong educational opportunities.

Musical behaviors are natural and vital parts of the living process; therefore the procedures of music education should be consistent with that process. They should attempt to develop significant linkage between the nature of the art and human nature.

Discussion and debate about the nature and function of education have been continuous throughout our history; this represents an honest and deepseated concern for how we want to be. Charles Reich (1970) is one of many critics who have reflected on the widespread dissatisfaction with education as we know it. He wrote:

> The central American problem might be defined as a failure of education. We have vastly underestimated the amount of education and consciousness that is required to meet the demands of organization and technocracy. Most of our "education" has taught us how to operate the technology: how to function as a human component of an organization. What we need is education that will enable us to make use of technology, control it and give it direction, cause it to serve values which we have chosen. (p. 390)

50

Sometimes discussion about education has focused on self-development or the realization of individual human potential while at other times the emphasis has been on people's social condition and how education might better serve society. With an expanding population in a shrinking world, it makes no sense to consider man unless he is viewed in a social context, and so our primary educational goal must be to balance and integrate individual fulfillment with social growth.

This is no mean task. A moment's reflection on our own brief lives will produce examples of quests for personal fulfillment that have been stunted by communal demands or obligations. Similarly, it is not difficult to recall examples of the reverse situation where communal growth has been inhibited or stifled due to excessive demands for fulfillment by one or several individuals.

BALANCED EDUCATION

The balancing of self and society begins in the family; it is extended in the school, then in a vocation, and finally it reaches its ultimate challenge as we become responsible members of a particular community. At each stage there are opportunities for success and failure, opportunities to develop autonomous or automaton roles. There are challenges that can extend the self-image or hasten retreat into anonymity. We can become vital thinking, feeling, sharing human beings or we can become burnouts submerged in a world of unreality.

> Explore some general philosophical sources on education and attempt to determine whether the thrust is on individual fulfillment or social conformity. Reflect on your own education (in the broadest sense), and discuss the balance or lack of balance in your own growth up to this point.

The technocracy in which we live has brought with it vast challenges for human adaptability but some people have clung to values and customs of yesteryear. Other people have turned their backs on all but the most recent innovations, while still others, perhaps with a sense of desperation, have drawn from different times and places trying to find satisfaction in variety and composite life styles.

On the one hand we find ourselves faced with undreamt of opportunities for creative and exciting experience; while on the other we recognize just as many opportunities that are potentially destructive and negative. As a result, we are often stretched in opposing directions and our lives, our schools, and our communities become dangerously unstable. The instability seems likely to increase unless we can build and balance more meaningful links between individual

and communal experience. This must surely be the central focus of
education as we move towards life in a new century.

In 1961 Philip Phenix wrote:

> The most important product of education is a constructive, consistent,
> and compelling system of values around which personal and social life
> may be organized. Unless teaching and learning provide such a focus,
> all the particular knowledge and skills required are worse than use-
> less. . . . Our greatest danger is not the avalanche of novelties with which
> the industrial age presents us, but the loss of direction that exclusive
> preoccupation with the problems and pleasures of innovation entails.
> (p. 17)

Though our challenges are now those of a "high-tech" era, we
are still searching for that sense of direction in education: a sense
that perceives and strengthens relationships between different events,
between different but associated phenomena; a sense that allows us
to grasp the larger shapes and not be swept away in a flood of trivia.
When we perceive such linkages, we are in a better position to derive
meaning and make wiser and more humane choices in any endeavor.

The curriculum reform movement of the 1960s represented one
attempt to deal with the problems outlined above. It was hoped that
if many subjects were restructured in the school curriculum students
would gain a greater sense of how the component parts of a discipline
could relate to one another and contribute to the whole. Ideas and
principles fundamental to a particular subject were introduced at an
early age and re-visited and reinforced as students matured. "The
curriculum of a subject should be determined by the most fundamental understanding that can be achieved of the underlying principles that give structure to that subject" (Bruner, 1963, p. 31).

But in our enthusiasm for restructuring subjects, we tended to
minimize the tremendous significance of the students, the experience
repertoire they brought to school with them, and particularly their
perception of themselves in relation to curriculum subjects. The self-
image, the concept of one's own identity, is vitally important in the
educative process. Obviously students who feel success-oriented, based
on their own records of achievement, are more likely to succeed than
failure-threatened students; nevertheless, self-attitude is more profoundly complex than this. Students are potentially capable of relating
to subjects in the curriculum in many different ways. So much depends, however, on how that linkage is developed; so much depends
on how far a student feels he or she can enter into or invest in a
subject, and of course how much value is derived from experiencing
a particular subject.

If a subject is perceived to be of value to a society or a community, that is a positive thing. However, if students consider a subject to be valuable to themselves, this seems even more important in terms of motivation and learning effectiveness, particularly at earlier stages of development.

> What are some of the most formative educational influences that have contributed to your self-image? Consider both positive and negative input. Why do you think some subjects threaten your identity while others support and confirm it? Is this a function of the nature of the subject, the way it is taught, or the way you have come to know it?

Clearly we need to make the values of music education obvious not only with rhetorical eloquence, but in ways individual students can grasp. This is most likely to happen when the musical experience is educational and the educational experience is musical. Only then will the implicit and authentic relationships between subject matter and learner have opportunities to emerge. But before we examine the nature of this relationship in music education, let us consider the broader aspect of the arts in education.

ARTS IN EDUCATION

According to Jerome J. Hausman in *Arts and the Schools* (1980), "Three general characteristics need to be present in an effective arts program: 1) opportunities for personal identification and involvement with art forms, 2) help in developing understanding and/or control of artistic media and 3) knowledge of a broader context of artistic efforts by others (past and present)" (p. xiii).

The call here is for an attempt to balance the development of individual involvement with a sense of historical and stylistic perspective. Sometimes our schools have emphasized practical involvement with art forms in the sense of making music, writing poetry, or producing paintings; sometimes they have emphasized knowledge about art forms, such as theories, history, styles, genres, or distinguished composers, painters, and the like. In recent times, schools have approached the arts more analytically and students have been encouraged to increase their perception of the artistic elements and forms.

We face an enormous dilemma in teaching the arts. On the one hand, we have an ever increasing diversity of art forms available to us, each requiring extensive training, practice, and skill before we can approach individual mastery. On the other hand, we have an artistic history that spans a multitude of cultures, generations, and styles, involving massive amounts of material that can never be experienced in one lifetime, let alone in a brief school career. There is little enough time in school curricula for the arts and so crucial choices have to be made. There are those who say, somewhat despairingly, that we can do little more than expose children to artistic products by means of galleries, concert halls, or visiting artists. Others say somewhat disparagingly that the arts provide a welcome relief from the more vigorous intellectual challenges and should therefore not be taken too seriously: "A few songs, band at the games and contests, some pretty drawings, and maybe a play or two!" A third group accepts the challenge to do what is realistically possible given the real constraints that exist. They believe artistic experience is a basic human need, essential to the development of whole human beings; they believe the primary function of the arts in education is not simply to produce artists per se, but, rather, people who because of their artistic experiences know and enjoy more fully the living process, participating, sharing, and contributing more effectively within it.

The starting point and probably the most fundamental justification for arts in education is the artistic experience or the artistic process. The *qualities* of the artistic process must be addressed if we expect to involve students with art. Obviously if the artistic process is incomplete or lacking in integrity, the artistic product is bound to be found wanting; therefore, we need to balance our analyses of artistic products with a deep concern for the authenticity of the artistic process. What does this involve?

Jeanne Bamburger (1978) writes: "Research in the development of competence in the arts is in a peculiarly important position since, if it is done seriously, it can engage what is becoming a central issue in learning and development, namely, the investigation of internal or intuitive representations of knowledge and their relation to formal descriptions" (p. 174). Bamburger claims that "it is precisely because the arts lie in the intersection between intuitive experience and formal descriptions of it that I believe them to be such powerful even essential domains of learning" (p. 174). She defines intuitive knowledge as "the processes by which an individual makes sense of the world around him or her, determining the quality, value and meaning of his or her immediate experience" (p. 173).

This particular notion, with its emphasis on relatedness, allows us to draw together the properties of an artistic object and the production or consumption of that object in an educational context. The relationship is, in essence, a creative process which grows from a desire to give structure to individual experience. In *Time Regained*, Marcel Proust (1970) stresses that the lives of most people are encumbered by numerous "snapshots" of experience that remain quite useless because the mind has not developed them. It is very necessary that, at all ages and stages of growth, we should reflect on our experience; we should have opportunities to structure and recreate our experience in order to grasp the essence of who we are and what we are about. The arts should nourish that sense of self-identity; they should support a personal vision that can illuminate a larger arena. The visions of Beethoven, Shakespeare, and Michelangelo and thousands of lesser artists have helped all of us to know more clearly what we think, what we feel, who we are, and who we can become. Thus their self-expression, their sharing had enormous social value.

> Can you think of some examples that might illustrate the ways in which art can restructure personal experience? Then consider your own relationships with music and the extent to which your involvement with music allows you to restructure and perhaps clarify your experience. You may wish to define "experience" before you become too engrossed with the idea!

If the arts are going to be taught with an increasing emphasis on the integrity of the artistic process, we are going to have to understand the nature of creativity more fully and incorporate creative principles into our teaching strategies. Current thinking in this area parallels Bamburger's ideas in intuitive thinking and also our own emphases about the nature of music. Silvano Arietti (1976), for example, writes, "A creative work cannot be considered in itself only; it must also be considered in reference to man. It establishes an additional bond between the world and human existence" (p. 4). "Creative work thus may be seen to have a dual role; at the same time as it enlarges the universe by adding or uncovering new dimensions, it also enriches and expands man, who will be able to experience these new dimensions inwardly" (p. 5).

The need to draw inferences, to develop linkage between human experience and art objects, is apparent in so much literature it is surprising that we have not been more successful in implementing the idea in arts education programs. Some of the reasons for this are clear. First, we have clung to the idea that artistic products (the concerts, the exhibitions, or the plays) justify and sell the programs and so the ends have often become confused with the means, and true creativity has been replaced by imitation or an exercise in following the leader. Second, we have taught the arts as a body of knowledge or as a developmental skill rather than as a *process* that emphasizes personal exploration, investment, and fulfillment. Finally, we have assumed that the arts may be learned in much the same way as we learn other subjects in the curriculum, namely, by employing for the most part only logical, deductive, and analytical thinking processes. Creative, divergent, and intuitive processes have yet to be fully explored within the basic thinking, feeling, and sharing modes of learning. In other words, we need a clearer focus on the basic nature of the artistic process and we also need to be more innovative in how we teach the arts and how we encourage students to learn the arts. We need a deeper insight into ways of linking the artistic process to teaching and learning processes. If our teaching and learning strategies are divorced from the fundamental nature of the subject we are in trouble. But if our teaching and learning processes are embedded in the subject and grow naturally from it, then we are most likely to achieve our goals. Charles Leonhard and Robert House (1972) have written, "Possibly the most recurrent error in the past has been the failure of instruction to remain consistent with the nature of the art" (p. 76).

Let us then consider one particular art, namely music, and how it can fulfill a valid and exciting educational role via instruction that "remains consistent with the nature of the art," and with human nature as well.

MUSIC IN EDUCATION

There have been many diverse roles and goals for music education through the years. These have ranged from an emphasis on recreation, self expression, and understanding other arts and cultures, to the development of moral and spiritual values and the satisfaction of aesthetic needs. Undoubtedly many of these goals will continue to be espoused or revisited as we move into a new century; however, the goals that are likely to receive most attention are those based on the needs of human beings in their social environments. Therefore, music education should be perceived and taught in ways that will develop significant linkage between tonal phenomena and human experience.

Charles Gary (1975) summed up this viewpoint quite succinctly when he wrote, "The purpose of music education in our time is clear; to reveal to students what music can do for their lives and to offer as many opportunities for musical learning as they desire and are capable of assimilating" (p. iii).

For us to move toward this goal we cannot merely teach the subject, we must teach the child as well; we must build bridges between the *sound phenomena* that are in the music and the *experience of music* that is in the child. That crucial linkage consists of behaviors—musical and human, external and internal—that take place in an educational setting. It is these behaviors that can make a musical experience educational and an educational experience musical. Both components are essential to complete and give life to the cycle, for students to derive meaning and value from their experiences.

Reflect on your own educational experiences and try to determine which were primarily subject matter oriented, which were
primarily student oriented, and which seemed to achieve a balance between the two extremes. Can you recall any specific teaching strategies that assisted linkage between the subject and your
own particular stage of growth?

Successful music education programs have always attempted to
achieve a balance between student and subject matter concerns, but
there are too many examples where this balance has never been achieved
and perhaps never even sought. Some of these latter programs have
attempted academic respectability perhaps, by presenting knowledge
of music without the related experiencing of music. Other programs
have provided students with extensive opportunities for making music
without developing an understanding of why they were doing it, nor
of the human experience and value potentials associated with it.

Some of our most musically competent teachers become frustrated
because the more dedicated they are to the cause of music and to
teaching it, as they understand these things, the more students appear
to turn away from the subject. These teachers often resign in desperation or somewhat cynically attempt to entertain their students,
but in either case the crucial linkage between students and music is
unrealized. If that linkage is to develop, music must be perceived and
taught as an art form that provides opportunities for individual exploration, investment, and growth at all ages. The quickest way to
stifle the artistic process is to remove opportunities for individual
involvement or imply that artistic choices are limited to moral judgments of right or wrong, good or bad. Students need to explore
alternatives. Their curiosity needs to be stimulated by searching out
new possibilities which in turn encourage new relationships to develop.

Students must be able to perceive value in their relationship to
music and music education. This requires meaningful interaction. Brainstorm ideas for involving young people in the exploration of their own needs and the ways in which various musics
may meet those needs.

Such development does not take place in an overly structured
classroom with tightly sequenced activities; nor does it happen in a
classroom that floats without direction or careful evaluation. It happens in a balanced atmosphere of constraint and freedom, control
and creativity, an atmosphere that is consistent with the ideal nature
of music and humanity. If the balance is to be achieved, there has to
be a commitment to very careful planning, teaching, learning, and

evaluating, processes that are themselves closely akin to artistic and life processes.

The terms planning, teaching, learning, and evaluating are key terms in any educational endeavor. Consider each term and discuss its meaning and implications for music education. You may not wish to define the terms, but at least consider the parameters of their operation and the ways in which they relate to one another.

SUMMARY AND PREVIEW

Let us consider each of these areas—planning, teaching, learning, and evaluating—in turn as a summation of part I, "Principles of Music Education," and more particularly chapter 3, and as a preview-overview of part II, "Processes of Music Education."

In terms of *planning* there is an obvious need for greater efforts to differentiate between behaviors that are phenomenologically based and those that are psychologically based. We need to use vocabularies that are valid for both areas and to employ them with care and consistency in our planning and follow-through. A vocabulary that is derived from musical phenomena will focus on the physical, formal, and aesthetic properties of sound events. A vocabulary that is derived from experiencing musical phenomena will focus on the psychological processes that take place within as the musical events unfold. A third vocabulary is needed to focus on the educational behaviors that link the phenomena with the experience of the phenomena; that is, behaviors that link the music with the student, behaviors that include a variety and blend of thinking, feeling, and sharing. With these three vocabularies in action, we will be in a stronger position to ensure that our planned educational experiences are indeed musical and our musical experiences are in fact educational.

Music *teaching* begins most generally with an aural and/or visual diagnosis of student musical needs. These needs or problems may reside in one or more of three areas: the technical, the conceptual, and/or the expressive. These are the areas that teachers must diagnose, either separately or in combination. Sometimes a diagnosis is straightforward and direct, for example, when an instrument is being held inappropriately, or a rhythmic pattern is poorly articulated, or a performance lacks stylistic authenticity. On other occasions, a diagnosis may include several problems or concerns that arise simultaneously in a group situation; but the order in which a teacher chooses to handle them could very directly affect the degree of progress that might be achieved toward their resolution.

> View a videotape of a lesson, class, or rehearsal, and try to de-
> termine the number of concerns that are diagnosed in each of
> the above categories. The teacher's verbal and nonverbal be-
> haviors should provide the key to those concerns.

When a diagnosis has been made, a teacher can select verbal or
nonverbal behaviors or a combination of both to handle the situation.
If the choice is primarily verbal, then there is the question of what
vocabulary is appropriate and also whether the verbal directions should
be in the form of questions or statements. If the choice is nonverbal,
a teacher's behavior may involve musical modeling, modeling with
the body by means of gesture or movement, or perhaps singing syllables to provide an aural image of the music. Some teachers' behaviors are a complex kaleidoscope of verbal and nonverbal strategies
reinforcing one another in rapid-fire sequence, while other teachers
select a narrower range of behaviors in order to meet the problems
they have diagnosed. The relationships that develop between musical
concerns that are diagnosed and ensuing teaching strategies determine a teaching style that obviously has considerable import for learning effectiveness.

> View another videotaped lesson and concentrate on the verbal
> and nonverbal behaviors of the teacher. Do verbal and nonverbal
> behaviors reinforce one another? Does one behavior tend to
> dominate? What kinds of vocabularies are employed? To what
> extent does the teacher provide a model for what is desired?

Learners as well as teachers have the option of verbal and nonverbal
behaviors. These will be considered in three categories, thinking,
feeling, and sharing modes, all of which involve verbal and nonverbal
dimensions. If the thinking mode of learning is operative, the primary
focus involves identification, comparison, and organization of the
musical events and experiences; it represents a rather ordered process
and is linear in character. The feeling mode of learning is more loosely
structured and involves intuitive and imaginative leaps between what
is recalled, what is, and what has yet to be. When we feel music we
are probably more concerned with the psychological than with the
phenomenological response, but not exclusively so. We need to remember that feeling and thinking are not mutually exclusive attributes; they may coexist or succeed one another with quite remarkable
alacrity. In one moment we may be analyzing and comparing while
in the next we may be deriving some form of imagery or metaphor
from the musical events, or simply immersing ourselves within the
tonal-rhythmic flow.

We also learn by sharing music nonverbally and by sharing our
thoughts and feelings about music verbally. This domain of learning

is frequently limited to a one-directional flow from teacher to student or students, but we need to develop opportunities to reverse that flow and also to provide opportunities for student to student sharing, both verbal and nonverbal.

Consider your own learning behaviors in music and the extent to which thinking, feeling, and sharing modes have been employed. Has one mode tended to dominate at one age or at one level of instruction? Why do you think this may have happened?

If these modes of learning are actively encouraged in music education, the quality of human experience is also enhanced. When people interact with one another at depth levels in an artistic process they develop new perspectives on and insights into themselves as well as into those with whom they interact. Musical learning is encouraged and the living process is enriched.

Education has been charged with many responsibilities over the years. Those responsibilities today are awesome. The human condition and the social order at times appear quite disoriented and alienated from each other. As a result persons of all ages have a great need to explore and extend their creative and imaginative lives in ways that improve their self-image and provide positive interactions with others. The arts can help meet these needs if their essential integrity and the students' personal integrity are preserved in the educational process. This can only happen if we provide opportunities for students to enter into the artistic process, to become involved with artistic phenomena by thinking, feeling, and sharing those experiences that challenge them to see themselves as they have been, as they are, and as they may yet become.

While *evaluation* and accountability may be overemphasized at times, such instances or eras often are a pendular response to an earlier lack of effort in these matters. Such extreme vacillations tend to occur when we consider evaluation as an end in itself, rather than as a part of a process. The purpose of the evaluation ingredient in the education process, in the music process and the life process itself, is not merely to acquire a set of critiques and assessments for the sake of assessment, not to have mounds of data for the sake of number games, nor is it just for grades. Casual observations, self analyses, professional diaries, needs assessments, videotapes, behavior charts, knowledge test data, performance critiques, teacher and program appraisals, attitude scales, aptitude and achievement measures, statistical procedures, and the like, all can be highly useful tools that can help to complete the vital feedback loop in the educational process.

In fact, without evaluation there is no smooth, efficient educational process, particularly if orderly progression is an essential aspect.

The process simply cannot flow and cycle effectively from planning to teaching to learning and back to planning without the feedback information that evaluation provides as a basis for further planning. Indeed, some feel that the entire process should begin with evaluation and needs assessment. "Summative" evaluation of general accomplishment to assess levels of goal attainment and for grading purposes is important, but we believe that "formative" evaluation for the purpose of making more specific diagnoses of strengths and weaknesses in an effort to further instructional planning is even more essential. Unfortunately the latter seems less well known and less well practiced.

Evaluation must be concerned with the student, the teacher, and the program. Student evaluation is anchored on the concept of the musically educated person, and evaluation of musical learning ultimately must be couched in terms of human behaviors evoked by and with music—how effectively students grow as human beings via musical experiences. We should be concerned with ability to produce music, but also to understand and use music effectively, to use it as a wise consumer, for humane personal and social purposes. Knowledge, skills, and attitudes provide the basis for thinking, feeling, and sharing behaviors.

We need to stress also that teacher and program evaluation are as essential as student evaluation. Again, however, these seem less well known and well practiced. Of course, since the learner, teacher, and program are interactive agents, evaluation of any one component reflects on the others as well. However, it is important that we attempt to assess these admittedly nondiscrete variables as scrupulously as possible to further the formation of effective music education practices and musically educated human beings. Life without valuing and evaluating would tend to be meaningless, quite dangerous, and probably disastrous! So would the life-enhancing process of education.

We conclude this chapter on education by stating explicitly what has been implied throughout: Education and educators are the most vitally important elements in our society today. Resources for education and the socioeconomic status of teachers may not always attest to that fact, but the fact remains: Education holds the hope for the future and is the essential factor in human development and social progress. Holistic music education can and should play a basic role in this development of thinking, feeling, sharing, humane beings.

EXTENSIONS

Statements

1. "We take the position that the school, and music education, must become more sensitive to social processes and take a more vigorous part in

directing social change. . . ." Music Educators National Conference, *Documentary Report of the Tanglewood Symposium* (Washington: MENC, 1968), p. 111.

2. "It is education itself that lies mired in trivia, prejudice, chronic measurement diseases, and all the rest, waiting for leadership which is so busy with management that education is largely forgotten." Goodlad, John I., "Beyond the Rhetoric of Promise," in *Arts and the Schools*, ed. Jerome J. Hausman (New York: McGraw-Hill, 1980), p. 215.

3. "Those who teach the arts should recognize the existence of many art forms and should be aware of change in the world of arts. Arts courses must not be bound by rigid definitions of the medium, time of creation, or culture from which the art emerges. The traditional curriculum consisting only of courses in visual art and music is no longer sufficient. Other arts should be recognized as valid components of learning, and however the arts are redefined arts education should adjust accordingly." Rockefeller, David, Jr., Chairman, *Coming to Our Senses: The Significance of the Arts for American Education* (New York: McGraw-Hill, 1977), p. 249.

4. "All art is metaphor. It takes one part of your experience, and another part of your experience, and it forces you to look at them together. And by this act of looking at them together, the work of art makes you see each experience afresh and differently." Bronowski, J., *The Visionary Eye: Essays in the Arts, Literature and Science* (Cambridge: MIT Press, 1978), p. 16.

5. "What makes for creativity is not any unconscious outpouring, but the process whereby carefully selected and arranged elements of such fantasies are rigidly worked over by a critical mind in a most disciplined way within the framework of a well-understood tradition." Bettelheim, Bruno, *Surviving and Other Essays* (New York: Vintage Books, Random House, 1980), p. 414.

Questions and Suggestions

1. If we thought of education less in terms of levels of abilities and more in terms of significant personal and social interactions involving imagining, searching, sharing, and combining, what effects would this have on music education?

2. What criteria are involved in making choices about the kind of education that is valuable and appropriate? How do you know you are getting a good education? Do you establish your own educational goals and evaluative criteria, or does someone else do that for you?

3. In what respect has your education been most successful to date, most exciting, or most satisfying? Why? In what respect has it been least successful or most frustrating? Why?

4. Why is there confusion about values in the arts? Is it because the arts fulfill so many functions?

5. Should art (including music) education serve a social and/or individual conditioning function or process, or should it serve a role of reflection and commentary? Can it do both? How?

6. Discuss your perception of the primary thrust of the arts at different levels of the school system. What would your priorities be in selecting arts curricula and arts experiences for different situations, for example: an inner city elementary school, a rural high school, or a suburban junior high school?

7. Discuss the role of the music and art critic in contemporary society.

8. How important is the intent of the artist or composer when it comes to deriving artistic or musical meaning and value?

9. Try to recall a learning experience in which you were deeply involved with the artistic process. Describe the characteristics of that process in detail and the extent to which you believe it reflected the true nature of the art form.

10. How do you think the functions of music have changed in our society? What are some of the factors that have influenced that change? Give examples for the past and present.

11. Is it reasonable to argue that with a plurality of musical functions in society, music in education should also represent a plurality of functions?

12. Should music education attempt to relate music of other societies to music in our own society? If so, how?

13. What conclusions can be drawn about man's need for music in American society? What is your evidence?

14. We have many musics in society: Western, non-Western, popular, contemporary; with many functions: educational, for entertainment, patriotic, religious, commercial, and so forth. How do these forms and functions relate to one another? Devise a model that might illustrate their common qualities without destroying their unique qualities.

15. In your journal, make an analysis of your own music education. Try to determine the weighting of skill development, knowledge, and musical meaning and aesthetic response. What kinds of activities and experiences were related to each area?

16. Where have we been least successful and most successful in providing the creative mind with opportunities for action and fulfillment in the music program?

17. Is all music artistic? Should we concern ourselves with nonartistic music in education?

18. When does music become social studies rather than musical studies?

19. Discuss the implications of creative and re-creative behaviors in music education.

20. Discuss three kinds of musical experiences that you feel characterize creativity in music education. Justify your choices.

21. Discuss (a) the reasons and (b) the means for providing greater scope for a student's imagination and feelings within a music curriculum. Illustrate your answer by making reference to particular programs.

22. What makes a musical experience educational?

23. Discuss the following statement: If musical performance is to realize its full potential and meaning within the curriculum, there must be a better balance between musical athletics and musical aesthetics.

24. List and develop arguments you would use to support a greater measure of individualized instruction in music education.

25. Develop reasons to support or refute the view that music in education must do more than simply reflect music in society.

26. Is popular music more significant socially than musically? What impact is your answer likely to have on the music program you structure?

27. How would a general sensitivity to the social foundations of music education be reflected in a music education program?

28. Discuss the relationships, the areas of conflict and resolution between music in society and music in education.

29. To what extent should music in society determine music education practice? List and discuss your principles as they relate to this matter.

30. Re-examine the Marcel Proust idea presented in the "Arts in Education" section of this chapter. What might he mean by the notion that snapshots of experience are useless unless developed by the mind? That experience must be consciously related to the self to have meaning? That if awareness is not developed, we remain trapped in a blindly enculturated, habitual life-style? Would Proust agree that, while the mind and intelligence cannot act on that which has not been felt or experienced, feeling is not of much human value in and of itself—until it has been contemplated, understood, and appreciated?

31. Most of us and most of our students live most of our lives interacting with the commonplace aspects of the real world. Should our music classes be more concerned with this real world or with the possibilities and experiences of a more ideal world—one best evoked through the arts? Should this be an either-or question? Consider: Is it redundant and wasteful to deal with the commonplace in school? If we do not deal with the commonplace, do we convey the false impression that the commonplace is neither important nor worthwhile? Yet, common experiences often are what composers develop and enliven with their creative insights and techniques to provide more meaningful, heightened experiences. So, can we help students to use music effectively in their quests for ideal experiences as well as for real-life applications enhancing and elevating the numerous daily activities that music can enliven and enlighten, make more meaningful and enjoyable? Is one aspect more important than the other? If so, which, and why?

REFERENCES AND READINGS

Arietti, Silvano. *Creativity: The Magic Synthesis*. New York: Basic Books, 1976.

Bamburger, Jeanne. "Intuitive and Formal Musical Knowing: Parables of Cognitive Dissonance." In *The Arts, Cognition and Basic Skills*, edited by Stanley S. Madeja. St. Louis: CEMREL, 1978.

Bruner, Jerome S. *The Process of Education*. New York: Random House Vintage Books, 1963.

Choate, Robert A., ed. "A Philosophy of the Arts for an Emerging Society." In *Music in American Society: Documentary Report of the Tanglewood Symposium*. Washington: Music Educators National Conference, 1968.

Dewey, John. *Democracy and Education*. New York: Macmillan, 1916.

Gary, Charles L. "Why Music Education?" *NASSP Bulletin*, vol. 59, no. 393. Reston, Va.: National Association of Secondary School Principals, 1975.

Hausman, Jerome J. *Arts and the Schools*. New York: McGraw-Hill, 1980.

Kaplan, Max. *Foundations and Frontiers of Music Education*. New York: Holt, Rinehart and Winston, 1966.

Leonhard, Charles, and House, Robert W. *Foundations and Principles of Music Education*. New York: McGraw-Hill, 1972.

Madeja, Stanley S., ed. *Arts and Aesthetics: An Agenda for the Future*. St. Louis: CEMREL, 1977.

Mark, Michael. *Contemporary Music Education*. New York: Schirmer Books, 1978.

Moytycka, Arthur, ed. *Music Education for Tomorrow's Society: Selected Topics*. Jamestown, R.I.: GAMT Music Press, 1976.

Mursell, James L. *Human Values in Music Education*. New York: Silver, Burdett, 1934.

Phenix, Philip H. *Education and the Common Good*. New York: Harper and Brothers, 1961.

Proust, Marcel. *Time Regained*, translated by Andreas Mayor. London: Chatto and Windus, 1970.

Reich, Charles A. *The Greening of America*. New York: Random House, 1970.

Rockefeller, David, Jr., Chairman. *Coming to Our Senses: The Significance of the Arts for American Education*. New York: McGraw-Hill, 1977.

Taylor, Harold. *Art and the Intellect*. New York: Museum of Modern Art, 1960.

Tellstrom, A. Theodore. *Music in American Education*. New York: Holt, Rinehart and Winston, 1971.

Thompson, Keith P. "How the Arts Function as Basic Education." *Music Educators Journal*, April 1977, pp. 41–43.

PART **II**

Processes of Music Education

Processes: Methods of operation; continuous proceedings; progressive forward movement; going through orderly developmental stages; methods for accomplishing specific purposes; states of becoming.

It is important to keep before us the realization that processes are not products, that a process is not an end in itself, even though a product might be the ultimate end of a process. Processes are *states of becoming*. When we consider educational processes, we are concerned with progressive forward movements that are truly continuous proceedings, because we recognize education as a life-enhancing and lifelong activity. Therefore, in a real sense, life is also a *state of becoming*, and the nature of education is congruent with the nature of life—as it should be.

In formal education we attempt to help students by organizing programs in orderly developmental stages and by implementing methods for accomplishing the specific purposes that are the goals of schooling in a democratic society. Of course, our ultimate goal must be to enable students to maintain the educational process beyond their years with us, for all of their years. In helping them become independent of us, become autonomous learners and self-developers, we reaffirm the continuity and congruity of life and educational processes. This is particularly important in music education where we face the criticism that school music activities too often end with school. Thus our major challenge is to plan programs and teach so as to enable our students to continue to develop themselves and share of themselves as musical persons throughout their lives.

To accomplish this our processes must be rooted in principles; they must proceed from a foundation of congruent beliefs about mankind, music, and education itself. The consideration of such principles in part I of this book has led us to realize that the processes of education must be consistent with the nature of music and mankind and has led us further to identify four essential processes that provide the topics for the chapters that constitute part II.

Recognizing that we are not dealing with totally discrete processes, and furthermore that there is continual interaction among the processes in effective education, the chronological flow of procedural emphases for an experienced teacher might be *planning, teaching, learning,* and *evaluating.* However, the logical and particularly the psychological order of presentation in teacher education programs at various levels might be somewhat different, both in terms of subject matter familiarity and order of need. Certainly preprofessionals in their early field work and even in the early stages of student teaching or interning seldom are immediately responsible for basic planning and evaluation. Generally they are initiated via formal classroom observation and gradual involvement in the teaching-learning processes, planning and evaluation being assumed only as later responsibilities. Also, it is helpful for any teacher to know more of what music learning and teaching processes involve before attempting to plan for and evaluate them. Thus, in this text the processes of music education will be considered in the order of *teaching, learning, planning,* and *evaluation.* In using the text, however, the chapters may be ordered in any manner deemed most appropriate to the needs of the class or seminar involved.

Now let us proceed to the processes, keeping in mind that processes are not products but *states of becoming.* In the same sense, music education is not an end in itself, nor is there such a thing as "music for music's sake." Students may not be used or abused "for music's sake." Music has no sake as such. Music is for man's sake, and the valid processes of music education, those grounded in valid principles, can lead students to man-music interactions that will enhance a lifetime of humane growth and development.

4

Teaching

Underlying Concepts: Teaching requires a willingness to view music in a human and social context as well as an aesthetic context. Because music is defined in terms of thinking, feeling, and sharing, the primary goal of teaching must be to stimulate growth in these areas.

Teaching involves the diagnosis of student needs and the selection of strategies, styles, and materials to meet those needs.

Teaching requires a repertoire of nonverbal strategies including modeling and demonstration abilities, and verbal strategies including professional, behavioral, and experiential vocabularies. There must be a well-developed capacity to phrase questions and make meaningful statements, as well as to express meaningful nonverbal behaviors.

Personal and organizational management skills are an essential adjunct to efficient and effective teaching.

What do we need to know about teaching? Certainly more than any book can contain. However, this chapter emphasizes several of the most basic topics, along with several other matters which should be basic but are too often slighted in teacher preparation. The content of this chapter on teaching is based firmly on the belief that "Teachers are born, not made" has no real validity. Teachers can be taught to teach, just as surely as they hope to teach others.

The chapter follows the natural flow of the text thus far. To illustrate, let us briefly introduce the subsections: "The Students" and "The Music" are applications of the "Man" and "Music" chapters that launched the text; and the rest of the chapter concerns education in terms of the other essentials of teaching. Specifically, *diagnosis* relates to planning and emphasizes our contention that the music teacher must be a diagnostician every bit as much as the medical doctor or a good auto mechanic. Diagnoses result in *concerns*, problems relating to students' goal attainments, which are broached via musical activities enlightened by *verbal* and *nonverbal* teaching behaviors. These behaviors are often slighted, particularly in music teacher development, because music is essentially nonverbal and thought to speak for itself. But, if music simply speaks for itself, why music education at all? In fact, verbal and nonverbal skills may be even more important to effective music education than to many other fields. *Congruency* among teaching behaviors, content, and student needs is essential, as is a repertoire of *teaching styles*. The latter is often thought to refer to the way a teacher operates most naturally, intuitively, or comfortably; but again there is much more to it than that: A variety of styles must be learned and available within the teacher's repertoire for use as determined at any moment by various program goals and student needs. Finally, the matter of *management* is considered in terms of interpersonal relationships, motivation, program development and maintenance, and public relations. Such personal and organizational skills are essential to effective education.

THE STUDENTS

We need to know our students: Where they have been, where they are, and where they may be going. We need to know their interests and aspirations, likes and dislikes, attitudes and values. We need to know this information about individual students as well as groups of students. We deal with a wide range of behaviors. Some students are warm and gregarious, others appear cold and indifferent; some are enthusiastic, committed, and sincere, while others are tentative, bored, or disruptive.

We need to realize that students learn a great deal outside of school and before formal education even begins. This is especially true of music with regard to such things as rudimentary vocal skills, rhythmic responses, and expectations concerning tonal and harmonic tendencies. In many cases more music is learned, for better or worse, from outside agencies such as the media and disc jockeys than from formal schooling. Formal education must take into account informal education.

It is usually easier to nourish an interest in music than to create an interest. Nevertheless music teachers are called upon to do both. We need to recognize talent and aptitude and to discover uniqueness, but we also need to work with students who have no special interest or aptitude in music to see if we can send them off humming!

The better we know our students as people, the greater the opportunity to work with them as music students. At the risk of being overly obvious, the need to know our students as individuals most certainly extends to the exceptional children with whom we work in or out of our regular classes. Mark (1978) states that "exceptional children are the ones whose abilities, because of physical, mental, or emotional abnormalities deviate sufficiently from normal children to require special and/or modified educational experiences" (p. 218). However defined or categorized, be they learning disabled, gifted, physically handicapped, or a host of other appellations, they are thinking, feeling, sharing persons, with the same basic needs for friendship, respect, encouragement, love, and individual concern that others have. It should be noted that many exceptional children function well in regular music class environments and require a minimum of alterations in content and teaching styles. (The references to Mark, Bessom, Graham, Duerksen, and MENC [1972] at the end of this chapter are particularly helpful in providing detailed information in this regard, and the specific pages indicated are recommended as required reading.)

As we begin to know all of our students, we begin to know what they are capable of bringing to the music class or the rehearsal. This is very important because music requires a degree of self-investment. The concept of sharing one's self through the musical experience is particularly significant. Music teachers view the experience of music as an opportunity for human growth. That is, we regard musical behavior not simply as the production or perception of tonal phenomena, but also as the response to those phenomena. Music challenges us to think carefully, to feel deeply, and to share ourselves generously. Music challenges us to structure and become aware of our feelings, to enjoy subtlety and to value sensitivity.

THE MUSIC

While we need to know our students, we also need to know our music, but what does knowing music mean in this context? Does one have to know the history of music, be an ethnomusicologist, play all the Bach preludes and fugues or be familiar with a dozen opera libretti? Of course one does not have to be a surgeon to teach anatomy, nor does one have to be an astronaut in order to teach astronomy or a Van Gogh to teach painting, but in order to teach any of these things successfully, there must be an ongoing absorption with the subject, a deep enjoyment that leads to further inquiry and discovery. People who teach music usually know something of its history, something of its theory, and can play or sing to some extent, but these are minimal qualifications. Obviously the more teachers know about the subject, the more resourceful teachers are likely to be. We need music teachers who are well grounded in many aspects of the subject and who are capable performers. We also need teachers who are articulate about music, teachers who are willing to share their musical insights through a vivid vocabulary and imaginative modeling.

Such verbal and nonverbal teaching skills will be the subject of detailed examination as we proceed through this chapter, but think for a moment how important it is to communicate and share values. Can you describe the kinds of words you use when you want to share a rewarding experience with someone? How many of the chosen words might be called expressive? Do you get excited when you use these words, and does your voice become more expressive than usual? And what about your gestures? Your face will probably become animated and you may use your arms or hands for emphasis. You try to capture the heart of the experience, those things which you valued most. (This may be termed a pre-artistic condition: Feelingful voice modulations can lead to music, just as body gestures, expressions, and hand-arm movements can lead to dance and drama.) We should feel like this frequently when we teach music. Expressive words and gestures need to be a vital part of our basic teaching equipment; they are a bridge between the sounds of the music and the thoughts and feelings of the students.

To teach really well we have to have two loves—music and students—and we have to know how to bring them together. It is not enough to love one without the other. We operate in a reciprocal and mutually supportive arrangement in which students invest something of themselves in music and are in turn nourished by it, having needs fulfilled through the interaction.

You may wish to consider in what ways the role of a music teacher differs from the role of a musical entertainer or a music therapist. Do some entertainers teach in or through their performances? What do you think of the ideas that music therapists work to make ill people well, while music educators work to make well people better? Or that the music therapist uses music to help people and the music educator helps people to use music? Perhaps you may differ with the ideas that have been presented here and you may wish to travel a different road. Can you suggest other roles for a music teacher? How would they affect classroom behaviors?

DIAGNOSIS

With a strong commitment to students and to music, we are ready to teach. The first step is one of diagnosis. Again we are faced with alternatives: Do we diagnose students or music? Again the answer must be, both! What do we look for?

First, we need to gain a more detailed picture of our students, starting with general attitudes and moving to more specific behaviors and musically oriented abilities. Which students appear to be success-oriented and which are threatened by failure in music? Positive and negative attitudes soon manifest themselves but we must try to determine possible causes of polarization. Have some children had poor music instruction? Perhaps negativism is the result of parental pressure or being forced to make difficult choices about the use of time. If we observe children's physical, social, and emotional behaviors in and out of the classroom, we can often gain insights into the kinds of musical problems they may have. We can also gain insight from other teachers and counselors. This kind of diagnosis and insight frequently speeds musical growth. A purely musical diagnosis may not reveal underlying causes, human problems, and needs, and thus musical progress will be impeded.

Because many music classes are large, in-depth individual insight is often difficult to achieve; nevertheless it should be stressed again and again that to teach a subject is to teach a child and the more that is known about the child, the more successful the teaching is likely to be.

> Think of some emotional and social characteristics in your own personality. How may your musical growth have been impeded or accelerated by those characteristics?

There is another kind of diagnosis that is more specific than what we have termed general attitude, but it is not yet a diagnosis of performance skills or musicianship. It has to do with musical aptitude, talent, or potential, and the matching of activities and instruments with the individual students. You may have met people who in their own words "cannot carry a tune in a bucket." They frequently claim to be tone deaf. Other people describe how futile and frustrating their efforts have been in music until they discovered the "right" instrument or musical activity.

Some research indicates that musical aptitude may be regarded as a highly variable commodity made up of several separable skills such as melodic, rhythmic, tonal, and harmonic perception. Some people are stronger rhythmically than melodically and vice versa. Fortunately, all of these abilities can be developed and improved upon with practice so that no one need feel permanently handicapped in music.

Music teachers need to be aware of and make judicious use of diagnostic tests, preferably standardized tests, of musical aptitude.

The resulting data can provide some reliable bases for advising students about which classes to take and which instruments to study. A student who is rhythmically weak cannot be expected to make rapid progress playing tympani or snaredrum, nor can a melodically weak student excel readily on a stringed orchestral instrument. Some students who demonstrate high musical aptitude may not have considered musical studies and, conversely, students with low aptitude may have been blaming their teachers or instruments for lack of rapid progress. For example, if a specific weakness in rhythmic or tonal discrimination had been known, then the problem could have been isolated for special attention. It is obviously very important to match student abilities with specific requisite skills in order to ensure maximal growth and minimal frustration. Of course, we must remember also that great enthusiasm for a particular instrument or activity may yield motivation strong enough to overcome known weaknesses related to that activity, in which case even a mismatch can yield significant learning and progress.

Do you feel your musical education has ever been hindered because of inappropriate instrument choice or voice part placement? How long did it take to determine the error, and who made the diagnosis?

If students are happy with their instrument choice, the type of group in which they are performing, or the music class they are in, but are still frustrated with their progress, then the next level of diagnosis should focus on the musical literature that is being employed. The literature may be inappropriate in terms of difficulty, but it may also be inappropriate in terms of the musical or aesthetic meanings inherent in the compositions. Students need to be challenged by the literature, but they also need to be rewarded. A judicious balance is necessary if progress is to be maintained. It sometimes takes courage to set aside a composition that has been rehearsed for several weeks, but if frustration or boredom outweighs progress, then it is more reasonable to select other materials.

Our attempts to know students have taken us from a general attitude assessment, through an evaluation of musical aptitude, to the choices of performing media or music classes and the choice of music literature. All of this is preliminary to making a diagnosis of student musical behavior. Clearly, if background information is known, then diagnosis is likely to be more accurate and effective.

CONCERNS

Now we can imagine we are in a classroom. We know quite a lot about the students both musically and nonmusically and we have certain expectations for the lesson or the rehearsal we are conducting. We have scheduled a series of musical experiences as part of our planning procedures. Shortly after the start of the lesson our expectations are not fulfilled; if it happens to be a really bad day, those expectations may even be shattered. We call a halt because we are concerned, and our concern is likely to fall into one of the following categories: technical, conceptual, or expressive. The concern may have been anticipated in the planning stages of the lesson but on the other hand it may not have been considered. Many things happen in a lesson or rehearsal that have not been planned. That is why it is important to think of concerns as immediate or spontaneous goals. In fact, they are likely to constitute a significant part of teaching time in any lesson.

Concerns represent a drawing together of student needs and musical needs. It is possible to think of student needs as being separate from musical needs outside the context of the music classroom, but when you are in the classroom and the situation is alive, both sets of needs have to be dealt with and that is why the term *concern* best expresses what has to be done.

Consider some specific examples: You are conducting a beginning string group in a junior high school and you notice an extraordinary diversity of bowing in the violins; your concern is technical. You are teaching a song to a fourth-grade class and you hear several children singing an interval inaccurately; your concern is primarily conceptual (although there also may be some technical aspects present). You are preparing the opening number for a spring band concert but there is no vitality or drive to the attacks; your concern is expressive. You are teaching a solo instrument but you hear faulty intonation and you see poor finger positions and poor posture; your concerns are both conceptual and technical. You are teaching a listening or music appreciation lesson to sixth-graders and you ask them to recognize repeated tonal-rhythmic patterns by raising their hands when they hear one, but only one-quarter of the class responds at the appropriate moment; your concern is conceptual. (Of course there may be a more basic attitude, attention, or motivation problem here, too!)

Consider the relative weighting of a teacher's diagnoses. Some teachers diagnose problems in each of the three categories many times within a single lesson. Other teachers diagnose in one category for protracted periods of time. Sometimes teachers give their students a detailed rationale for a diagnosis but at other times they simply diagnose and move straight into remedial strategies. How often do you provide rationales for your diagnoses? Perhaps you approach this whole area somewhat differently by asking students to diagnose their own musical behaviors, or you may ask them to provide rationales for the diagnoses you make. If this happens, the level and quality of interaction is certainly likely to increase within a lesson.

Sometimes we diagnose many problems in rapid succession, bombarding our students with technical, conceptual, and expressive concerns to such a degree that student self-esteem may be severely threatened. On other occasions, we do just the opposite, as though our diagnostic skills were paralyzed, and we resort to repetitious rehearsal in the hope that particular passages will improve or particular problems will evaporate.

Another feature of diagnosis relates to the degree of complexity involved. A problem may be simple or compound but a complete and detailed diagnosis does not necessarily have to be revealed nor acted upon at one time! For example, an expressive concern may involve conceptual and/or physical problems that should be diagnosed and dealt with before the expressive concern is addressed. Of course, on the other hand, if a physical or conceptual diagnosis is not at some point related to an expressive need, then the end results may be less than musical.

On some occasions our diagnoses are limited to musical concerns when in fact we need to reach beyond to diagnose a human problem. Under these circumstances the musical problem is unlikely to be resolved unless the human problem is first diagnosed and attended to. Diagnoses are not a simple matter if we consider the sources, the frequency, the variety, the complexity, and the rationales involved.

Generally, it is best to deal with concerns as they arise, otherwise there is the obvious danger of continuing to practice and thus reinforcing the wrong response. Sometimes several concerns may arise almost simultaneously. Then priorities need to be established and choices made. We need to be sensitive to student needs particularly if we approach the students' overload point and they begin to feel inadequate to the task. We can all recall teachers who never seemed to be satisfied with our progress or even our efforts.

Now let us consider each area of concern in greater detail. First, the *technical* area. Here we are dealing with something that looks wrong or awkward or inappropriate; it may be a body position such as the wrist, the fingers, the arm; it may be the shape of the mouth, the position of the head, the facial expression or, in the case of an organist, it may even relate to the feet. Then we may also observe the body in relation to the instrument. Where is the instrument held? How is it held? Are the physical movements on the instrument smooth and effortless? Concerns in the technical area tend to dominate during early instrumental lessons and possibly again at very advanced stages when a master teacher may diagnose subtle technical movements with the precision of a fine workman, or even that of a surgeon if something needs to be removed!

Technical concerns may also occur in teaching music reading, music theory, improvisation, or composition, but the primary focus in these areas is more generally conceptual and is concerned with the development of the "inner" ear or the musical imagination. Subcategories in this area relate to what is heard rather than to what is seen, so we are dealing with intonation, articulation, phrasing, voicing, balance of parts, harmonic densities, dynamic schemes, modulations, cadences, rubato, and so forth. Such concerns and their related terminology are well known to professional musicians but less well known to beginning music students. Therefore, if we have conceptual concerns, we need to be sure our students are familiar with the related vocabulary so that they may understand and respond to expressions of such concerns.

> Try to recall some of the concerns expressed during the most recent rehearsal of your performing ensemble. Make a list of the conceptual concerns. Now imagine yourself in an elementary classroom. How many of those same concerns might arise and under what circumstances? If you were the teacher would you modify the vocabulary while still focusing on the same concern? If so, how?

Expressive concerns may develop in the band, orchestra, recorder group, piano class, chorale, stage band, listening class, or movement to music group, or any other music class for that matter. We are concerned here when students seem to have missed the musical message. Some teachers would say they "hear notes but no music." Students are not projecting meaning or are not responding to meaning; somehow the music is remote and impersonal; there is no self-investment or self-realization through the sounds. Climaxes are dull, subtlety is lost; we can anticipate everything! Conversely, we should not forget the possibility of excessive expression, perhaps a flamboyant carefree showmanship that destroys stylistic integrity and becomes something of a selfish indulgence. Extremes are to be avoided; the goal is expressiveness that is dramatically conceived and delivered at the culturally and socially appropriate level of subtlety.

> Can you recall how some of your own teachers have communicated concern in the expressive area? Probably some have humored you; possibly some have screamed at you; some have reasoned; and some have pleaded with you. How would you handle an expressive concern if you were conducting a very good high school choral group? Share your ideas.

We have already alluded to the dangers of sharing too many concerns too quickly with students. To offset this danger it is sometimes helpful to encourage students to voice *their* concerns. They may be identical with our own, or they may highlight a feature that has escaped our attention. In any event, students will often listen to their peers more attentively than to teachers. For this reason alone, it is sound practice to encourage students to voice their concerns.

Probably as teachers we all have our favorite concerns. Some of us listen more for conceptual than expressive problems while others are quite expert in diagnosing technical matters. Superior teaching must surely take into account all three areas as a student develops. Indeed, musical growth is bound to be inhibited unless reasonable balance is maintained among the three areas.

VERBAL BEHAVIORS

Apart from making music or listening to it, talking about music becomes the next best means for acquiring a musical education. Talking about music in conjunction with making it or listening to it provides the most potentially powerful educative process. Because of this the particular vocabulary that is employed in the process of education can be a vitally significant influence on the quality of education. Therefore we will consider three distinctive vocabularies that can be employed to assist the educative process: the professional, experiential, and behavioral vocabularies.

The *professional* vocabulary has as its primary function to describe the tonal phenomena as accurately as possible. It is helpful to think of tonal phenomena as possessing three basic properties: physical, formal, and aesthetic. A professional vocabulary that deals with the physical properties of sound and its production might include such words as vibration, intonation, articulation, intensity, legato, duration, attack, release, or timbre. A vocabulary dealing with formal properties would include melody, rhythm, harmony, syncopation, or crescendo as well as reference to such things as coda, binary, rondo, or symphony. Aesthetic properties could include words such as shape, color, unity, balance, variety, space, design, pattern, or line. (See figure 4.)

An *experiential* vocabulary balances what is heard and perceived with what is felt. It describes the individual response to tonal phenomena. This is an intrinsic part of the educative process because it helps to build bridges between students and music. An experiential vocabulary may be intensely personal in that it deals with covert behaviors that are complex and transitory in nature but are nevertheless very real. When we use an experiential vocabulary we are attempting to articulate the meanings derived from the musical events. The vocabulary brings together what is heard with what is felt, what is imagined and what is sensed, what is analyzed and what is reflected upon. The vocabulary may be in terms of an image such as an event, a place, color, shape, or person. It may be in terms of a metaphor dealing

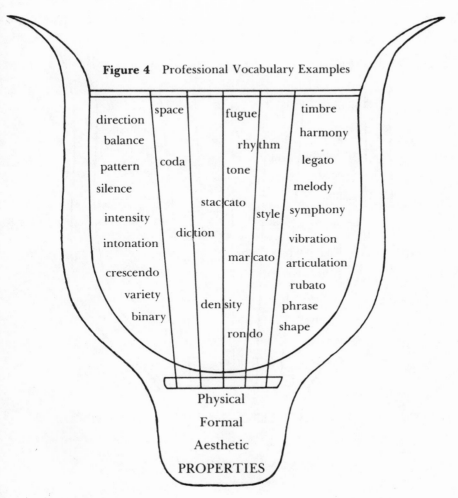

Figure 4 Professional Vocabulary Examples

direction
space
fugue
timbre
balance
rhythm
harmony
pattern
coda
tone
legato
silence
melody
staccato
intensity
style
symphony
diction
intonation
vibration
marcato
articulation
crescendo
rubato
variety
density
phrase
binary
shape
rondo

Physical

Formal

Aesthetic

PROPERTIES

with a quality of feeling or a quality of movement such as eager, calm, or energetic; or, alternatively, it may relate to the living process and include such words as growth, decay, distortion, cohesion, gravitation, stability, tension, or relaxation. (See examples in figure 5.)

Our third vocabulary is termed *behavioral*. It indicates the kinds of potentially educative behaviors students exhibit when they interact with music, behaviors that vary from highly cerebral intellectual analyses through an intense range of feelings to some generalized social interactions or communications. A behavioral vocabulary reflects the gamut of human capacity to respond in a multitude of ways that can be broadening and self-educating. Three subcategories of behavioral vocabulary are thinking, feeling, and sharing. (See figure 6.)

Thinking behaviors are characterized by individual linear, system-

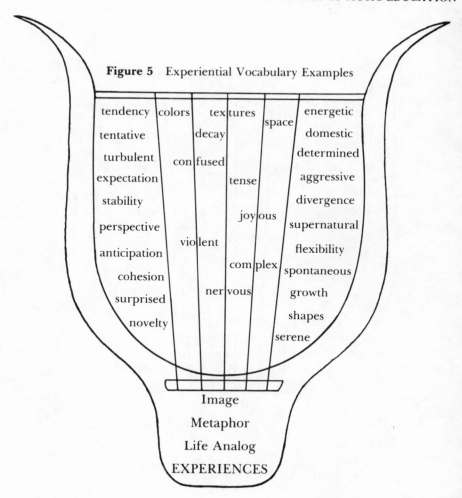

Figure 5 Experiential Vocabulary Examples

tendency colors   tex|tures
                            space   energetic
tentative   decay   domestic
turbulent   con|fused   determined
expectation   tense   aggressive
stability   divergence
                     joy|ous
perspective   supernatural
            vio|lent
anticipation   flexibility
                   com|plex spontaneous
cohesion
            ner|vous   growth
surprised
            novelty   shapes
                             serene

Image

Metaphor

Life Analog

EXPERIENCES

atic, analytic, sequential, convergent processes. They include analyzing, defining, comparing, relating, and identifying, to name just a
few. Feeling behaviors are frequently characterized by individual nonlinear, spatial, intuitive, imaginative, spontaneous, divergent, generalized processes. They include sensing, exploring, imagining,
discovering, inferring, elaborating, and so forth. Sharing behaviors
are characterized by social, interactive, dynamic, communicative,
give-and-take participating processes. They include demonstrating,
performing, describing, explaining, rehearsing, asking, interacting, and expressing. These types of behaviors are not mutually
exclusive or clearly definable acts; rather they indicate an emphasis
or desire for one learning behavior rather than another in a given
circumstance.

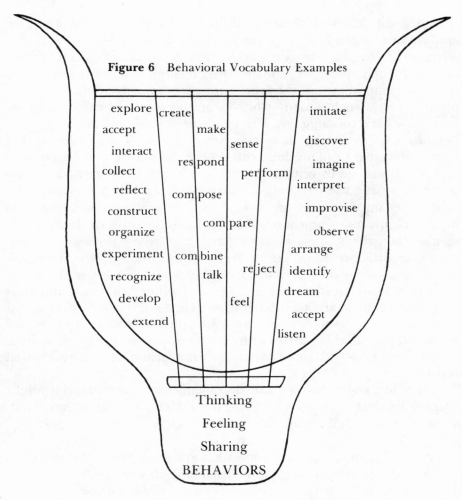

Figure 6 Behavioral Vocabulary Examples

explore create
accept
make
interact sense
res pond
collect per form
reflect com pose
construct
com pare
organize
experiment com bine
talk re ject
recognize
feel
develop
extend

imitate
discover
imagine
interpret
improvise
observe
arrange
identify
dream
accept
listen

Thinking

Feeling

Sharing

BEHAVIORS

> Think of some musical events you have been involved with re-
> cently. Try to decide if your behaviors there were oriented more
> to thinking, to feeling, or to sharing.

It is important when you are considering the emphasis on verbal
communication skills in this book and when you are developing these
essential skills for your own teaching, to remember that words are
not totally unlike music. That is, while we often think of words as
communicating exact information, what *we* mean, they generally have
a component of ambiguity that, while not as great as in most music,
still is sufficient to permit their artistic employment. For example,
poetry is the artistic use of words that may involve the reader or
listener personally, aesthetically, and creatively precisely because of
the ambiguity of the verbal content.

What this leads up to first and foremost is the fact that when we employ in this book, and in our teaching, words categorized as descriptive of physical, formal, or aesthetic properties; image, metaphor, or life-analog experiences; or thinking, feeling, or sharing behaviors, we must remember that these are categories of convenience and emphasis, that in reality many word meanings tend to bridge and flow from category to category. For example, the word *choose* in some persons' experiences or in certain contexts may be associated with a rather objective thinking behavior where the choosing is based on a highly rational set of criteria. For others it may be more of a feeling behavior where the choosing is based on subjective preferences. So it becomes important in our verbal communicating about music, as in all of our communication, that we consider our students as we choose our words. This is particularly true when we wish to communicate with precision. Of course at times some of our communications may take on an element of the poetic, for example, when dealing with metaphoric experiences or feeling behaviors, and thus they may result in artistic modeling as well. As a final caveat, it would be advisable to keep alert to terms and phrases unique to the contemporary youth subcultures with which we are working because these might provide us with some particularly useful and meaningful verbal resources.

Here are some examples of statements and questions you might employ in your classroom utilizing the different vocabularies. First, some examples that emphasize a *professional* vocabulary:

Bring a stronger sense of articulation into your performance.

Why do we have breathy tone quality in this song?

Identify and justify the point of climax in this phrase.

What are the factors that contribute to a sense of unity in this composition?

Describe ways in which the variation is achieved here.

Improvise a short variation for this rhythmic pattern.

Locate some examples of syncopation on your score and explain how they affect the design of the music.

Now some examples involving an *experiential* vocabulary:

Can you make this music flow?

This section sounds very chunky.

You need to whizz through this piece like a rocket.

The contour of this melody is quite angular.

There was a devotional quality about that performance.

Your playing sounds somewhat dry to me.

Here is a piece of music by Schubert that may make you feel
scared or nervous or frightened.

Let's see if we can float across the bar line instead of jumping on
the downbeat.

Did you sense a churning, creepy quality in this section of the
music?

Here is a piece that is full of energy.

Can you create a sense of relaxation when you project this phrase?

We must maintain momentum at this point so that the vitality is
not inhibited.

Here are some examples of statements and questions in the *behavioral* area. First, thinking behaviors:

Compare these two patterns and identify ways in which they are
similar.

Can you recognize a dynamic scheme in this section of the work?

Compile a list of sound sources you hear on this taped excerpt.

Now some feeling behaviors:

Vary the dynamic scheme in this music so as to bring about some
unexpected or humorous effects.

Imagine you have just been caught by a monster; which of these
musical excerpts would best tell your friends how you are feeling?

Discover your favorite sound on this instrument and then match
it with one of these picture portraits.

Finally, some sharing behaviors:

Discuss your reactions to this listening excerpt.

Demonstrate how you would conduct this measure.

Clap this pattern for the whole group.

Try to express the character of this musical phrase with a brief
gesture, a facial expression, or a single word.

If you consider these three vocabularies for a moment you will
realize they can very easily be used in association with one another
so that we may have a statement such as: Sing (sharing behavior) the
phrase (professional vocabulary) as if you were floating off into the
distance (experiential vocabulary). Or you may ask a question such
as: "Which of these orchestral excerpts would you select to accompany
this photographic sequence?—explain your choice." Here the students would be challenged to think, feel, and imagine with linkage
between tonal phenomena (professional vocabulary) and photographic sequence (experiential vocabulary), and then share their behaviors by justifying their choices (behavioral vocabulary).

You probably have realized that questions may be used to involve students more directly and more intensely than is possible with the use of statements only. They may serve a variety of functions. Questions may be quite simple, involving memory, such as: "What does this time signature mean?" They may involve reasoning, such as: "Why is the main theme delayed until measure 154?" Or they may call for a creative or divergent response such as: "How would you feel if the solo in this section were performed on a trumpet instead of a flute?" Some questions require judgments to be made. For example: "Does this solo represent clear examples of baroque performing practice?" Obviously questions need not be limited to the stimulation of thinking. Questions can and should challenge us to think, to feel, and to share.

The importance of verbal behavior extends beyond what may be said to the way it may be said. The quality of articulation can dramatically affect the impact of the message. Music teachers perhaps more than other teachers should be sensitive to this matter. There are three basic variables in speech articulation—tempo, pitch, and dynamics. They are also basic variables in music. Certain combinations in static groupings can create adverse conditions in the classroom. For example, the combination of low pitch, slow tempo, and soft dynamics will soon induce boredom or sleep. On the other hand, a combination of loud dynamics, high pitch, and rapid tempo will tend to set persons on edge and create a tense atmosphere. Variation in vocal delivery is desirable in all situations. Student teachers need to experiment with their own voices in order to find maximum impact.

Listen to a brief tape recording of a music class and analyze speech patterns in terms of dynamics, pitch, and tempo. What were the related effects?

Another variable that can influence vocabulary usage is the learning context. Teachers must be sensitive to different ethnic minority groups who are likely to have unique vocabularies, dialects, or methods of articulation. A wise teacher will weave some words from these vocabularies into the music teaching situation. This would be particularly appropriate in a lesson involving non-Western musics for example, but the practice need not be limited to those occasions. Similarly, there are bound to be opportunities for expanding vocabulary usage when working with special children such as the physically handicapped, the emotionally disturbed, or the blind.

Consider your own verbal potential as a music teacher. Do you possess a comprehensive and vivid vocabulary to draw on? What are some of the things you might do to improve your ability in this area?

NONVERBAL BEHAVIORS

Music is a nonverbal art. It follows that the way of knowing and understanding music must certainly involve significant components of nonverbal communication. Probably most of our nonverbal communication in music teaching has been casual or spontaneous, apart from conducting, which of course makes an art out of communicating without words. It is therefore appropriate to give more detailed thought to this aspect of our professional behavior and the impact it can have on teaching and learning.

Nonverbal behavior with the body or a part of the body provides a visual model and as such can be helpful to a learner. A conductor or musical director is perhaps the most obvious example of nonverbal modeling in music education. By a vast array of gestures a conductor is able to communicate and shape musical events ranging from huge and dramatic climaxes to subtle and precious moments. A conductor has a repertoire of gestures to match his repertoire of scores. Such gestures are not for the most part spontaneous or spur-of-the-moment movements. They require careful planning, rehearsal, and refinement if they are going to achieve maximum impact. It is important to note that conducting gestures convey not only information about the tonal phenomena, but also information about the conductor's response to those phenomena. In a sense, therefore, a conductor employs a silent vocabulary that is both professional and experiential.

Nonverbal modeling may involve intentional demonstration with parts of the body, perhaps in relation to an instrument such as a modified position of the bowing arm, the shape of an embouchure for a trumpet player, a diaphragmatic expansion for a singer, or a finger movement for a pianist. This kind of modeling has to do with sound production and is often directly related to technical concerns.

A teacher may also employ nonverbal behavior growing out of a conceptual concern to reinforce a melodic contour, to stress a harmonic density or cadence, to clarify a rhythm, or perhaps to provide a tonal image. Then there is the more challenging area of nonverbal communication in the expressive area. Here, the body can illustrate a quality of feeling or some characteristic movement perhaps, or a more abstract thought such as growth, conviction, or energy.

You can improve the effectiveness of your nonverbal communication by selecting and conveying concerns in brief score excerpts. The excerpts and concerns should be contrasting in nature. Take turns in communicating the essence of those excerpts to the other members of the class. You may choose a technical concern, a conceptual concern, or an expressive concern, but you will need to consider the amount and quality of body move-

ment you are going to employ. Maybe you will use just your
face, or just your left hand, or perhaps you will involve your
total body. If the members of the class do not get the message
readily, then you will want to practice more!

Body language has not been the subject of careful analysis until quite
recently, but if used carefully and in association with appropriate
verbal language, it can certainly offer strong support for effective
teaching.

Probably since the beginning of time, musicians have made use
of another kind of modeling: a cross between humming and speaking,
something that might be called syllabizing. Where no words exist,
neutral syllables become a means for articulating what is imagined
inwardly. Conductors, teachers, and performers frequently resort to
syllables such as da, da, dee, da, dum(!) to clarify the musical image
and to provide an aural model of what is desired. The process probably comes down to us from early childhood when we had all kinds
of imaginary rhythmic and melodic fragments floating into and out
of our minds; they were not yet identifiable compositions but they
reflected an ability to hear sounds in advance of their production.
This method has become a direct and economical means of communicating nonverbally and noninstrumentally because no highly
technical skill is required; simply a desire or willingness to share and
a vivid repertoire of sound syllables to draw on. It may be noted,
however, that this technique has been elevated to a jazz art form called
scat singing.

In the classroom or rehearsal room a teacher can save large amounts
of time by providing an aural model with appropriate oral syllables.
Developing this technique may require some concentrated practice,
as do any other teaching and performing techniques; however, it will
be well worth the effort because syllabizing brings a precision to communication about music that is sometimes quite difficult to attain if
we rely solely on verbal descriptions.

Syllabizing need not be the sole responsibility of the teacher. Students can be encouraged to think creatively and divergently when
they share their perception of a musical event via syllables. Furthermore, willingness to share on this basis can provide valuable insights
to assist the diagnostic process. By syllabizing a particular event, a
student may reveal a mistaken rhythmic perception or a different
sense of phrasing. On the other hand, a student may reveal an exciting
new approach to interpretation that can lift an entire rehearsal and
provide a foundation for genuine sharing and discovery.

The point needs to be stressed that just as verbal behavior is a
two-way street with questions and statements, so too is nonverbal

behavior. Students as well as teachers should be involved in nonverbal communication as an aid to education.

> You can practice your skills in syllabizing just as you can in other forms of modeling. Take, for example, the same excerpts you used for the earlier nonverbal exercise. If each student in the class syllabizes an excerpt, these can be taped successively and you will be amazed at the diversity of syllable vocabulary and delivery style. It is best if students practice the excerpt on their own and then syllabize individually in isolation, so as not to be influenced by one another at first. Analyze and discuss one another's efforts.

Another form of nonverbal behavior occurs when a teacher actually plays or sings a particular passage, providing both visual and aural images. "If you hold the instrument like this" . . . or, "if you breathe like this" . . . or, "if you finger like this . . . then it will sound like this." Some teachers and some methods of teaching rely on this particular method very heavily. Other teachers probably never provide this kind of modeling. Some students may even assume that their teachers are incapable of playing an instrument or singing.

Musical modeling can be very effective if a student is motivated to imitate a teacher. The modeling may focus on technical, conceptual, or expressive areas, or on all of these simultaneously. However, it should be noted that this kind of modeling may lead to superficial imitation unless other forms of teacher behavior parallel the modeling. There can be no guarantee that a student will observe only what is intended. So it is important to provide a clear focus for the model. Sometimes students may learn more by modeling for one another than by relying solely on the teacher's model. This, after all, is one of the reasons for section leaders in choirs, for seating in particular chairs in an instrumental ensemble, and for group instruction in general.

We do not know if musical modeling is more educationally significant in some situations than in others. For example, we have no research results to tell us whether modeling in technical areas is more effective than in expressive areas. However, it seems likely that various aspects of modeling effectiveness will be related to the age and stage of a student's development. Here, too, there is little research to rely on, but certainly, if the model is too remote or too dominant, students are likely to be bored or intimidated.

The following checklist (figure 7) provides examples of the various types of nonverbal behaviors discussed here, and may also serve an evaluative or analytic function as discussed in chapter 7.

Figure 7 An Evaluative Checklist for Nonverbal Behaviors

NONVERBAL BEHAVIOR	Low 1	2	3	4	High 5
SOUNDS					
variety of syllables					
pitch of syllables					
dynamics of syllables					
appropriateness of syllables					
intensity of consonant sounds					
intensity of vowel sounds					
use of student modeling					
teacher modeling					
FACE					
use of eyebrows and forehead					
focus of eyes					
mouth positions					
variety of facial expression					
facial relationships to other gestures					
(LOWER TO UPPER) BODY					
angle of head					
size of gestures (arms)					
direction of gestures (arms)					
intensity of arm motions					
independence of arm motions					
location of hands during gestures					
direction of hand motions					
independence of hands					
position of fingers					
movement of feet					
mobility of joints (neck, elbows, etc.)					
angle of total body					
body position and movement					
GENERAL					
continuity of movements					
precision of movements					
use of surrounding space					
relationship of syllables and gestures					
relationship of silence and gestures					
range of feelings shared					
intensity of feelings shared					
confidence					

EFFECTIVENESS SCALE

CONGRUENCY

The question of congruency between verbal and nonverbal behaviors is a fascinating one and reminds us of the old adage, "Do what I say, not what I do!" This situation occurs in music teaching when a teacher wants one response but unwittingly encourages another. The teacher may want a pianissimo but the conducting gesture is too large to suggest a pianissimo; the teacher may want a certain articulation but the modeling is not really what is imagined; or the teacher may say that a work is exciting but the nonverbal message, the facial expression, or the body stance does not support the verbal claims. Music is a symbol for much more than mere sounds. This very fact makes it difficult to teach really well. Little wonder that incongruities creep into our teaching strategies; little wonder that we sometimes shout loudly when we want the music to be played softly; little wonder if we say, "Forget the expression; just get the notes right!" Little wonder that we sometimes dictate rather than educate.

> Take turns conducting the class in a well-known song. In your gestures overemphasize a concern so as to induce an incongruity. Discuss the results.

Contradictions and incongruities are not excusable, for a mark of professionalism is consistent and reliable behavior. Students should be able to expect from their teachers careful diagnoses, clearly stated concerns, and verbal and nonverbal communications directed towards musically viable goals. These are reasonable professional behaviors that can be recognized, evaluated, and improved upon wherever necessary.

Perhaps one of the reasons we may have difficulties is due to our emphasis on teacher qualities rather than teacher actions. This emphasis seems to persist in spite of the fact that it is what a teacher *does* that is of primary importance, regardless of the various personal qualities he or she may or may not possess. Similarly it is what a dentist or a nurse or a lawyer does that really describes their professionalism. It would seem, therefore, that teacher training in music must address the areas of diagnosis and remediation more directly and in greater depth, always seeking out incongruities that impair educational effectiveness.

With the increased availability of audiovisual resources it should not be difficult to acquire banks of teaching profiles so that students can analyze the concerns and related behaviors of teachers in many varied situations. The ability to articulate a concern quickly and to deal with it by employing appropriate remediation lies at the heart of the teaching process.

TEACHING STYLES

Teaching styles may now be defined as the actions of teachers based on the relationships between their concerns and their chosen strategies for remediation. Teachers may employ one or two styles over a protracted period of time, or they may utilize several styles in a relatively short period of time. An example of the former might be where a teacher identifies technical concerns as the primary focus for one student for six weeks. During that time the teacher could use many statements and questions employing a professional vocabulary, but might also use a limited amount of body modeling. An example of employing multiple styles might occur in an elementary music classroom with several activities such as listening, playing instruments, and singing. Here all three basic concerns arise from time to time within a thirty-minute lesson. The teacher talks about singing softly and expressively and models the music. She also asks if students can recognize selected instruments in recorded excerpts (conceptual concern), and she has some children improvise an instrumental piece based on a poem studied in the language arts period (technical, conceptual, and expressive areas). She can include nonverbal body modeling here to reinforce a metaphoric vocabulary derived from the poem.

How are teaching styles determined? The answer lies largely in the goals of the lesson. The goals must be preselected to some extent, but they are likely to be modified based on the concerns that arise during the lesson.

It is well known that children process music very differently from one another, based on the kinds of persons they happen to be. This complicates things a great deal for the teacher, for while he or she may have two students at the same time with one major concern, each student may require a different set of teacher behaviors in order to deal adequately with that concern. The problem becomes even more complex in a classroom of thirty children with all three basic concerns represented as well as a number of subconcerns. All of this requires a host of different, swiftly shifting behaviors from the teacher, if learning is to be efficient and effective. The teacher must make many rapid decisions based on the priorities and the aims of a particular program; thus priorities and aims must be well known and firmly held in mind.

The most obvious determinant in choice of teaching style will be student response. If there is notable growth towards goal achievement, then the choice of style is probably adequate. It may not be the most effective, however, and some change in behavior or new focusing of concern may be in order. Ongoing experimentation is essential.

Other factors such as age of students, size of class, content of lesson, duration of lesson, and the location or physical context of the lesson will influence teaching styles. The precise nature and effects of such influences will have to await the results of more intensive research. At this time we can only make assumptions and explore hypotheses; but you can assist the whole process by systematically evaluating your own teaching styles.

MANAGEMENT

There is an area of a teacher's responsibility that extends beyond teaching per se, and includes the components of management and organization. We could certainly find examples of effective teachers who are poor managers, and poor teachers who are outstanding organizers, but it is clear that both skills—teaching and management— are essential to a superior educational environment.

In one very important sense, management must be concerned with what is called "time on task." Effective schools research (see Denham and Lieberman, 1980) has repeatedly demonstrated a direct correlation between "engaged" or "on task" time and the amount of learning which takes place in a school setting. A well-organized teacher with well-established priorities maximizes the time in which students are actively and effectively engaged with learning experiences and minimizes disengaged time. The latter is a condition that may result from instructional procedures that confuse or bore students, from discipline problems, or from untimely housekeeping chores and undue business such as wasting class or rehearsal time in inefficient passing out or collecting of music, checking instruments or uniforms, planning fundraising events and trips, and so on.

In the broader sense the concept of management goes well beyond what takes place in the classroom. In this sense management embraces four major areas of responsibility for the teacher, including human relationships in and out of the classroom, program development, care and maintenance of the equipment and facilities, and, finally, the public relations image.

It is helpful to think of human relationships apart from teaching although they are obviously a vital part of teaching too and are related at very basic levels. The reason for separating them at this time is to highlight those things a teacher can do apart from actual teaching. Those are the things that will assist the development of a positive atmosphere for teaching. Some classrooms and schools generate a highly positive ambience that is immediately noticeable to a visitor; others operate in what might be termed a neutral atmosphere, and there is regrettably a third category where teaching is attempted in spite of a strongly negative environment.

Music teachers should be willing and able to share their musical expertise by helping other teachers enhance their curricular offerings and by helping with music-related social situations. We must always remember that music does not and never did exist in a vacuum. It exists in a world of other related, and potentially mutually enhancing, activities, and the same is true in the school setting.

Make a list of five to ten specific ways in which the music teacher, as the school's music expert, can assist other school personnel in curricular and social matters. Share and discuss.

A music teacher who cares about other aspects of the school program apart from music is more likely to attract the support of colleagues and students than one who dedicates his or her teaching life to music as an isolated part of the curriculum. Reaching out to students and teachers not directly involved in music provides excellent opportunities for making clear the goals of the music program and being accessible to others to gain their interest, respect, and support. It is a process of communication involving vitality, persuasiveness, and qualities of endurance. If people, faculty and students, view themselves as part of a team and they know what is being done and why it is being done, commitment and efficiency are likely to follow. With this kind of attitude outside the classroom, cooperative endeavor and regard for the program is more easily fostered inside the classroom. Less time will be spent on reprimanding students with negative threats, and, instead, a sense of individual respect and mutual support will be nourished.

It is very important that students should understand why they are doing what they are doing. A sense of purpose is likely to increase their motivation and enhance the quality of the learning. Similarly, if a teacher can delegate responsibility, students will feel encouraged to "buy into" a program, thereby increasing their commitment to it.

Make a list of things you would be prepared to delegate within your music program. What are some of the things you could do to convince students you are interested in them as people as well as music students or simply performers?

The attitudes expressed here about human interaction provide a foundation for program development. Quite simply, the music teacher needs the support of his or her students and colleagues if the program is to achieve quality. That is most likely to come about if the participants are encouraged to evaluate the program and participate in goal determination, literature selection, and other kinds of musical experiences. This is not to say the students run the program, but simply that time spent in group policy making can be time saved in terms of more effective teaching and a more highly motivational learning environment. If students are uncertain about some procedures or aspects of the program, it is worthwhile setting aside time, perhaps outside of class, to explore and explain in depth the nature and purposes of the program, what it is for and about. The principle here is that basic plans should be prepared, shared, and discussed as much as possible and practiced by those involved in them and affected by them. This approach undoubtedly calls for personal qualities of patience, imagination, persuasiveness, enthusiasm, conviction, and humility on the part of the music teacher. These are the qualities that provide foundations for teamwork, which in turn provides opportunities for quality teaching and learning.

Some of us may not be very systematic about the care of instruments, other teaching equipment and materials, facilities, careful budget development and presentation, and so forth, but these matters impinge very directly on classroom management. Inadequate budget support, poor facilities, shortages of texts or instruments do militate against a positive educational environment. Thus the music teacher simply must accept responsibility for such business and take care of such matters efficiently and effectively.

If human interaction has been positive and a cooperative spirit has been fostered within the program and the school, then it is likely that a fair and reasonable budget can be established. Priorities will need to be drawn up. This is another area where student, parent, and teacher-colleague input can be helpful. External funding and/or community support can be a very sensitive subject and generally should be sought only for very special projects in order to relieve the regular line budget from sudden surges and the program from accusations of unfair or excessive demands and expenditures.

Public relations is sometimes viewed as something separate from the day-to-day running of the school program: as a kind of special promotional stance that will sell the program to the target population. That is not the view taken here. The image that is most desirable is an accurate one, derived from the three areas of management already discussed, namely, human interactions, program development, and maintenance. If these areas are operating effectively, then there should be no need for window displays; rather, it is a matter of keeping the community informed as to what is actually taking place, the program goals, and progress towards achieving those goals. And, again, it would be good to remember while keeping the public informed and involved, that the teacher's primary public is his or her students.

Many music teachers have assumed that if their groups perform at concerts and football games, this will help build a good public image. While this may be true in part, it does not deal with the total picture. People need to know the rationale behind choices within a program, choices related to goals, literature, scheduling, travel plans, and many other activities. Teacher management reaches beyond the classroom to keep people informed and to build support, which makes the act of teaching more effective. Sharing quality with a community develops a sense of pride and helps the music program become a valued educational opportunity.

What was done in your high school to keep your community informed about music education? What could be done right now in your college to improve its public image? How much might it cost in terms of time and money?

The concept of management involves organizational skills, social-motivational attitudes, and human values that are an essential adjunct to effective teaching. They are part of the total educational enterprise. They can be developed independently of teaching skills and yet they influence teaching effectiveness to a marked degree.

Sometimes management skills have been confused with teaching skills, and some highly successful organizers have been mistakenly identified as the most effective teachers. Conversely, we may find examples of fine music teachers whose efforts are inhibited or frustrated by poor management skills. In fact, these two abilities are interdependent, mutually supportive, and in need of ongoing development.

EXTENSIONS

Statements

1. "A major problem in arts education is that too many teachers have been trained rather than educated and, like the whales, perform on cue without the least idea of why they are doing what they are doing." Hanshumaker, James, "The Art of Recognizing Artistic Teaching," in *The Teaching Process and Arts and Aesthetics,* ed. G. L. Kneiter and Stanley A. Madeja (St. Louis: CEMREL, 1979), p. 233.

2. "In order to understand student behaviors, we must understand the determinants of behavior as they exist for the student at that time, not as the teacher thinks they should exist." Raynor, Joel, "Motivational Determinants of Music-Related Behavior: Psychological Careers of Student, Teacher, Performer and Listener," in *Documentary Report of the Ann Arbor Symposium,* Music Educators National Conference (Reston, Va.: MENC, 1981), p. 346.

3. "So often an entire music class is taught as if it really consisted of only one student of average ability. The fact is that every class includes stu-

dents with vastly different levels of musical aptitude." Gordon, Edwin, *The Psychology of Music Teaching* (Englewood Cliffs, N.J.: Prentice-Hall, 1971), p. 62.

4. "Since learning and problem solving depend upon the exploration of alternatives, instruction must facilitate and regulate the exploration of alternatives on the part of the learner." Bruner, Jerome S., *Toward a Theory of Instruction* (Cambridge: Belknap Press, Harvard University Press, 1971), p. 43.

5. "Artistic problem solving requires the capacity to capture various modes, affects, and subjective insights within a symbolic medium; direct training of this skill is perilous, but a good teacher can devise situations that will draw productively upon the child's various systems." Gardner, Howard, *The Arts and Human Development* (New York: John Wiley and Sons, 1973), p. 293.

Questions and Suggestions

1. Music teaching is a complex and often ill-defined process. Can you provide historical or philosophical reasons as to why this might be so?

2. Do you consider the roles of conductor, director, and teacher to be synonymous, similar, or very different?

3. What kinds of information do you want to know about the children you are going to teach? How are you going to get that information?

4. List some strategies you would employ to (a) motivate interest in a new composition and to (b) retain high motivation and application until goals have been achieved.

5. Can you recall from your own music education examples of mismatching musical values and music literature, or mismatching musical abilities and music literature? Describe the results.

6. To what extent is musical growth dependent on the successful matching of instrument and student? Give some examples of how you might determine the success of the match.

7. Develop some examples of how *you* would teach for musical meaning.

8. List some strategies for involving the musical responses and ideas of your students in the shaping of the music they are rehearsing.

9. Reflect on your own teachers and the extent to which their diagnoses of your musical behaviors were comprehensive. Did these same teachers generally acquaint you with the reasons for a particular diagnosis?

10. Select videotapes of two music teachers and compare their relative speeds of diagnosis, complexity of diagnosis, and range of diagnosis. Prepare an analysis for your journal.

11. Try to recall some of your most productive music education experiences. In your estimation was your productivity due more to accurate teacher diagnosis than to appropriate teaching strategies? Was it due to both of these factors or was it due to some other variable such as high extrinsic motivation?

12. What are some of the ways in which the concepts of comprehensive musicianship can be demonstrated in a rehearsal situation in a high school performing ensemble?

13. Give some examples of what you would do to encourage divergent rather than convergent thinking in a music lesson focused on listening.

14. If you find yourself teaching a student or a group of students who are technically accomplished but limited or inhibited in expressiveness, what are some strategies you would adopt to remedy the situation?

15. Develop an imaginary classroom dialog that on the one hand emphasizes the development of musical perception and, on the other, the development of musical response. How do the vocabularies differ?

16. Of the three vocabularies discussed here, professional, experiential, and behavioral, which do you feel most comfortable with and why? How are you going to develop confidence with the other vocabularies?

17. Review some examples of music criticism in your local press or in a national paper or periodical and compare the relative weightings of experiential and professional vocabularies. Review a student or faculty concert and pay particular attention to your choice of words. Share the results in class.

18. When next you receive a music lesson, take particular note of the kinds of questioning procedures your teacher employs. Does the questioning encourage reasoning, memory, or creative and imaginative responses? Plan a lesson of your own in which you utilize a variety of questioning procedures.

19. Is nonverbal behavior a significant part of your behavior? What are some of the things you might do to improve your nonverbal communication skills and thus more adequately prepare yourself for music teaching?

20. Think of a quality of feeling you want to share. Can you make an appropriate movement to express it? Ask a friend if he or she can understand the feeling you are trying to convey. Now think of another feeling and write it down in the form of a shape or design. See if your friend can translate it into a movement. Now do the same thing with a word you want to share.

21. Select a short musical excerpt. What kinds of shapes or lines or patterns would you draw to show what the music is about? What kinds of words would you select to tell what the music is about? How would you move your arms to demonstrate what the music is about?

22. Select a short passage from a choral or instrumental score; by means of gesture and syllabizing demonstrate the range of musical meanings you wish to realize.

23. If you have access to a video camera, arrange to have yourself taped to analyze the nonverbal components of your teaching style. Is your modeling limited to one area (e.g., hands and arms) and one concern (e.g., technical)? What degree of congruency is evident between verbal and nonverbal strategies? How frequently do your behaviors change or your concerns alter, and so forth?

24. Many of us feel inadequate or defensive about our ability to model musically, physically, or aurally. Why do you think this is so? If you play in an ensemble, evaluate the kinds of modeling that are employed for

educational purposes. Do the players model or is the modeling left entirely to the director? Now evaluate the same procedures in a classroom situation or a private lesson.

25. Make a cassette tape recording of a series of lessons, perhaps three at one age level with appropriate musical content, and three with another age level and different musical content. Listen to the tape and analyze the vocabulary usage. Is the teacher encouraging the behaviors you hope for? Is the experiential vocabulary vivid and varied? Is there variety as concerns questions and statements? Are there questions relating to one particular concern but not another? How frequently does the teacher syllabize, and on the basis of what concerns or subconcerns? Is it limited only to rhythmic syllabizing, or phrasing, or articulation?

26. Can you think of some examples of incongruency between verbal and nonverbal behaviors? You will probably have no difficulty if you view a beginning conducting class, but you might also consider some classroom teaching examples.

27. Suppose you have been teaching only for several months, but you have become dissatisfied with the impact you are having on the students. Develop a checklist that you could use for self-evaluation purposes.

28. Make some suggestions as to *why* and *how* you might vary the *pace* of a lesson and the *focus* of a lesson.

29. What are some of the behaviors one might expect to see demonstrated by an "aesthetically aware" music teacher?

30. Discuss some of the major variables that are likely to dictate a particular style of music teaching.

31. Long before P.L. 94–142 and long before "mainstreaming" became the byword for the contemporary education of handicapped persons, many exceptional students were mainstreamed into general music classes. Do you believe that handicapped children have the same basic needs as other children, and that their needs can be addressed effectively in music classes? Consider specific circumstances as you respond to these questions.

32. View two videotapes and compare the respective teachers' management skills. What proportions of their lesson times are devoted to management?

33. We have discussed at some length the importance of the concept of self-investment in the musical experience but is this also true for teaching? How much of yourself are you willing to invest in teaching music? How should this willingness manifest itself?

34. Following are transcripts of excerpts from actual music lessons and classes. Read each one carefully and analyze in detail the verbal and nonverbal behaviors that are employed:

    A.   Class Piano Lesson:
          T: O.K. Now I'm going to break this down the way I did the one Mary's working on, section by section. What's wrong in this first section?
          S: Well, I *thought* I wasn't holding the top note.

T: O.K. You are not holding it as badly as you were, but your
     hand is absolutely rigid (provides physical model with hand),
     so what I'm getting is (provides musical model on piano). It
     is like a clenched jaw. Everything is just biting down. You
     are biting down. Look at my hand (musical model). What's
     happening?

S: Your arm is rolling.

T: Yes, the hand is relaxed and moving. Your hand is absolutely
     locked so the sound is rigid and it sounds like you are hang-
     ing on to the last note. If you will roll off it, it will dissipate;
     it will have the sound of steam out of a tea kettle . . . you
     know, out and gone, instead of Uugh! It's cutting off with
     a glottal chop. You know what I mean by a glottal chop? It's
     a hack to the throat. Uugh . . . this kind of sound instead of
     ahhh. It should end on an exhalation, not a chop. Try again.

B.   High School Choral Rehearsal:
     (Teacher-director interrupts choir . . .)
     T: How many remember my instructions to the basses and the
          baritones? What did I ask them to do in this section? Any-
          body? Do you remember basses or baritones?

     S: Put a punch on that note.

     T: Yes. Put a punch. Right! Or an accent there. Now, I didn't
          hear it, guys. Were you doing it? See, if you were it's not
          coming through to me so I need a little bit more. Once
          again . . . (interrupts again) Why is it not coming through?

     S: It's too low.

     T: Yes, it's the lowest pitch in the choir; therefore you need a
          little more sound to come through.

C.   Studio Piano Lesson:
     T: Alright now, wait a minute. What do you think about those
          three measures? Were they going any place?

     S: It's boring!

     T: It was a little flat, wasn't it? There's a pull toward
          this . . . (provides musical model on piano). He has his little
          motif or his little tiny theme and he's putting it into a se-
          quence but the reason is to build some intensity. Well, on
          the piano you can make a little crescendo but not too much.
          Try it.

D.   College Wind Ensemble:
     T: Let's go there at 89 please. Here we go 1,2,3, breath (music).
          No no no! It's not *Ah* da da da da, but *Da* da da da da.
          Not *Er* da da da da, *Er* da da da da. Not da da da da *dah*
          either, but *Da* da da da da.
          Again, 89! Let's go. 1,2,3, breath (music).

No! It's not machine gun fire either! (Laughter from the group.)

O.K. urghrrah!!! We are going to get to a point here where we can flutter tongue, brrrrr, and that would be great! Clarinets, maybe you guys should study with them . . . they're doing it too fast. You're doing it too slow! One more time, 89 . . . 1,2,3, breath (music).

Good!!!

E.   Clarinet Lesson:

T: How many beats would the first note get?

S: Two.

T: Two! Oh! We have six/eight time. What gets one beat in six/eight?

S: Half note. No! Quarter note.

T: O.K., six/eight . . . now what does the top six stand for?

S: Six beats in a measure.

T: Right. What about the bottom?

S: (Silence)

T: Eight means an eighth note gets one beat.

S: (Student nods)

T: In two/four time how many beats to a measure?

S: Two.

T: O.K. Now there is a four on the bottom. What would that mean? What gets one beat?

S: (Silence)

T: A fourth . . . or a quarter . . . remember? O.K. A quarter note gets one beat in two/four time, so then you apply that to six/eight time with six beats to a measure and an eighth note gets one beat; so if an eighth note gets one beat, what would a dotted eighth get?

S: One and one-half.

T: Good!

F.   Class Piano Lesson:

T: Now, what's the problem if you play it as printed? . . . That is (musical model).

S: Because that doesn't lead on.

T: Of course. It sits there in little static chunks. Chunk . . . chunk . . . chunk. No connection, no sense of motion. Just like a series of rocks; lined up rocks (musical model again). Now that's grossly exaggerated!

S: Yeah!

T: But if you can practice with that lead in, that sense of always leading to the first sixteenth and then re-starting on the second one, then it will start to rattle (musical model).

G.   Elementary Music Class:
    T: (Group finishing echo rhythm patterns on drums) What's starting to happen?
    S: We're starting to play against you.
    T: So what do you call that in music?
    S: Rondo!
    T: Is that a rondo? That's just because we started rondo yesterday! What?
    S: A canon.
    T: A canon! What is a canon?
    S: A second part echoing.
    T: Yes. Can we do some free canon? I'll start first. Look out! Is it quiet? Are you listening? What?
    S: What's a free canon?
    T: What's a free canon? Who can tell him?
    S: It's like she'll just keep on playing and we have to imitate her.
    T: You're going to echo me and I'm not going to stop, so you have to be listening to what I'm doing. O.K. Ready? Go! (class plays)
    T: Oh Good! Once more, that was very good. I was making them hard. Can we keep it soft? I've put the dynamics on the board today. Start soft and get a little louder. If I get soft, you'd better get soft! Are you ready?

H.   Junior High School General Music Class:
    T: I'd like for you to look at these pictures so you have some idea as to what they are; and I think, since you are close enough, I'll tape them to the board. Sarah, do you want to help? Peter, can you see what it is? Let me show it to you close up and then it will be easier. O.K.? Now we have this one. If there are people in these pictures, consider how they might feel; and, whether there are people or not, I want you to consider how you feel when you see them. When you see the pictures, how do you feel? And then I'm going to play a couple of different compositions and some of you might want to match two or three pictures to one composition based on how the pictures make you feel. Some of you might not find a picture that matches at all and if so, that's O.K. because you might have a better idea of what kind of picture you should have. You notice I'm not telling you what's on these pictures. I'm going to let you decide for yourselves because I don't want anything that I might say to influence how you feel about them. Listen very carefully and just let yourselves go with the music . . . (T. plays first selection).
    T: O.K. Which pictures would match with that selection, Steve?
    S: The first two.

    T: Tell me what's in the picture.

    S: The horses.

    T: Why?

    S: Because when it gets louder they go faster.

    T: You feel that when the music gets louder, it makes you imagine the horses going faster?

    S: Yes.

    T: Which other one, Steve? This one? Can you think of any words that might describe the music that would also describe this picture?

    S: Angry . . . disturbed . . . excited . . . the music is jerky.

REFERENCES AND READINGS

Bessom, M.E.; Tatarunis, A.M.; and Forcucci, S.L. *Teaching Music in Today's Secondary Schools.* New York: Holt, Rinehart and Winston, 1980. Particularly, see pp. 193–207.

Bruner, Jerome S. *Toward a Theory of Instruction.* Cambridge: Harvard University Press, 1966.

Bruner, Jerome S. *The Process of Education.* New York: Vintage Books, 1963.

Colwell, Richard, ed. *Symposium in Music Education.* Urbana, Ill.: University of Illinois, 1981.

Combs, Arthur W. *Educational Accountability: Beyond Behavioral Objectives.* Washington: Association for Supervision and Curriculum Development, 1973.

Denham, Carolyn, and Lieberman, Ann, eds. *Time to Learn* Washington: National Institute of Education, 1980.

Duerksen, George; Cobb, Vivian; Gilbert, Janet; Johnson, Thomas; and Turk, Gayla. *Learning Packages for the Music Education of Handicapped Students.* Lawrence, Kan.: Department of Art and Music Education and Music Therapy, University of Kansas, 1981.

Epperson, Gordon. *The Musical Symbol.* Ames: Iowa State University Press, 1967.

Goodlad, John S. "Schooling and Education." In *The Great Ideas of Today,* edited by Robert M. Hutchins and Mortimer J. Adler. New York: Praeger, 1969.

Gordon, Edwin. *The Psychology of Music Teaching.* Englewood Cliffs, N.J.: Prentice-Hall, 1974.

Graham, Richard M. *Music for the Exceptional Child.* Reston, Va.: Music Educators National Conference, 1975.

Graham, Richard M., and Beer, Alice S. *Teaching Music to the Exceptional Child.* Englewood Cliffs, N.J.: Prentice-Hall, 1980.

Highet, Gilbert. *The Art of Teaching.* New York: Alfred A. Knopf, 1950.

Knieter, G.L., and Stallings, Jane, eds. *The Teaching Process and Arts and Aesthetics.* St. Louis: CEMREL, 1979.

Leonard, George B. *Education as Ecstacy.* New York: Delacorte Press, 1968.

Mark, Michael L. *Contemporary Music Education.* New York: Schirmer Books, 1978. Particularly, see pp. 218–257.

Mursell, James L. *Education for Musical Growth.* Boston: Ginn and Co., 1948.

Music Educators National Conference (MENC). *Documentary Report of the Ann Arbor Symposium: Applications of Psychology to the Teaching and Learning of Music.* Reston, Va.: MENC, 1981.

Music Educators National Conference (MENC). *Music in Special Education.* Washington: MENC, 1972.

Music Educators National Conference (MENC). *Toward an Aesthetic Education.* Washington: MENC, 1971.

National Association of Secondary School Principals (NASSP). *Student Learning Styles: Diagnosing and Prescribing Programs.* Reston, Va.: NASSP, 1979.

Paynter, John, and Aston, Peter. *Sound and Silence.* Cambridge: Cambridge University Press, 1970.

Schafer, R. Murray. *Creative Music Education.* New York: Schirmer Books, 1976.

Smith, Robert B. *Music in the Child's Education.* New York: Ronald Press, 1970.

Wehner, Walter L. *Humanism and the Aesthetic Experience in Music: Education of the Sensibilities.* Washington: University Press of America, 1977.

Weingartner, Charles, and Postman, Neil. *Teaching as Subversive Activity.* New York: Delacorte Press, 1969.

5

Learning

Underlying Concepts: Learning music is more than the perception or production of tonal phenomena; it is in fact a process of relating tonal phenomena to human experience.

Learning music involves linear and nonlinear behaviors as well as thinking, feeling, and sharing modes of development.

Qualitative musical learning, that which is meaningful and valuable, is dependent upon individual ability to develop multiple and depth interactions between musical events and the ways those events are experienced.

Perhaps the most important question we can ask in music education is: What should students learn in their music classes? If we were to ask different groups of students what they learn, we would probably get answers such as:

We learn to sing.
We learn to read music.
We learn about symphonies.
We learn about composers.
We learn about the orchestral instruments.

Sometimes we might get answers such as:

We learn to compose.
We learn what cadences are.
We learn how to conduct.
We learn what contemporary music sounds like.
We learn what African music sounds like.

But what if we were to have answers such as:

We learn to imagine music.
We learn to anticipate music.
We learn to respond to music.
We learn to remember music.
We learn to recognize music.
We learn to discriminate between different kinds of music.
We learn to understand why there are different kinds of music.
We learn to explore music.
We learn to create music.
We learn to talk about music.
We learn to interact with music.
We learn to value music.
We learn to relate music to our lives.
We learn to use music in different ways in our daily lives.
We learn how music is used to influence people's behavior.

This second group of responses is really dramatically different from our first group and implies a very different kind of music program. The difference is due to a confusion that exists between what we do in music and what we learn in music. In fact, we know of students who can "do" a great deal of music and yet have learned very little about it. Of course some students have learned quite a lot about music but still cannot do it! The dichotomy is real and so is the problem, for if we emphasize doing without learning, we are focusing on a product and ignoring a fascinating process. Admittedly this is a common problem in our cosmetic society but it cannot be condoned in education and it certainly cannot be condoned in music education where the process is the key to the product. Because both parts of each pairing—process and product, learning and doing—are desirable, there must be some kind of order or priority on which to base our doing and our learning.

Identify in your own words what it is in music that a child needs
to learn.

If we consider the kinds of learning outlined above, we can see that there is indeed an inherent order within them. For example, we learn to imagine music before we learn to compose it; imagining is a process or part of a process, and a composition is a product. Similarly, we need to learn to feel music if we are going to learn what cadences are, and we need to learn to anticipate music if we are going to learn how to perform or conduct music.

Certain kinds of learnings are essential to musical doing. As a profession we have not been remarkably successful in describing these learnings or in incorporating them into our music teachings. It is not enough to tell students to listen to music; we have to tell them what to listen for and how to listen, which means to say what to do with their minds while they are listening. We know the mind does more than receive sounds. The mind translates the sounds into music. How? If there were a simple answer, music education would present no challenge and no excitement. But there are many answers, many ways to learn music, and we all learn according to the kinds of people we happen to be. Just as there are teaching styles to suit certain diagnoses and certain concerns, so there are learning modes to suit certain goals and purposes.

The first of these modes is the thinking mode, the second is the feeling mode, and the third is the sharing mode of learning. Although the learning modes will be considered in this order for the sake of analysis and clarity, do not be misled into believing that they are discrete functions. One or the other may be emphasized at various times in our behavior, but there is also much interaction. In fact, thinking and feeling modes tend to parallel one another and generally precede the sharing mode. Thinking and feeling are internal inter-actions, interacting with one another as well as with perceived tonal phenomena. Sharing, on the other hand, is an external interaction, a projection of thought and feeling that presupposes some degree of learning. However, sharing brings its own learning mode that is just as important as thinking and feeling.

> Before we consider each mode in turn, ask yourselves how you learned the music you have learned. Were your learning ex-periences process-oriented or product-oriented? Have you learned more by doing than by gaining insight and information before doing? What kinds of learning processes do you feel most chal-lenged by and most comfortable with? For example, have you learned music best by analysis or intuition or a little of both? Can you give some examples?

THINKING MODE

If we are involved in a musical experience and wish to employ a thinking mode of learning, there are two questions that must concern us: first, *what* do we think about; and second, *how* do we think about it? Obviously we must have a focus for our thinking or something to think about so that we are not daydreaming. To help us do that thinking we also need tools: ways of thinking and methods of thinking.

When we think about music we are thinking about what we are hearing; we are thinking about the tonal properties, namely the phys-ical, formal, and aesthetic properties. Clearly this is too much to think about at one particular moment and so our thinking is selective; we make choices as to what we wish to think about. Some of us may select an aesthetic property such as shape and simply think about the shape of the music, how it changes its shape, and what makes it change shape. Others may select a formal property such as tone and think about the way one tone blends with another or contrasts with another. That kind of thinking may lead to thoughts about tonal production, the physical aspect of musical performance which involves questions about how the tone is being produced or modified. Thinking about tonal properties can be a depth experience or a shallow experience, it can be systematic and probing, or it can be casual and fleeting.

If we are thinking about tonality, for example, it may be of sufficient interest for some of us to know what key a particular work is in; knowing that the first movement of a particular symphony is in E flat major may be enough. Others may be interested in thinking about the tonal structure of the entire movement, tracing in detail moves to closely related keys or distant keys, sudden and dramatic shifts as opposed to smooth modulations, bridge passages, transitional material, reinforcement techniques for familiar tonalities, and so forth.

We can think about certain properties of a piece of music and how these parallel the form of certain aspects for our lives. For example, we may hear and think about dissonances and consonant resolutions, and reflect on our hungers and satiations or on our struggles and successes; but this begins to touch on the linkage and interactions between thinking and feeling which are discussed later in the chapter in sections dealing with sharing, meaning, and value. It is important to remember here, however, as we think about thinking per se, that in actuality it is not an isolated phenomenon but a mode that is generally in a process of interaction with feeling, a more holistic process with the potential for great mutual enhancement.

Another example of musical thinking might have to do with the physical aspects of a piano performance. Perhaps initially we may choose to think about the brilliant clarity of the playing but then we become fascinated by how the brilliance is achieved. We watch the pianist as well as listen; we think about the performer's body posture, wrist position, rotating forearm, high finger action; we think about use of the pedal and how sparingly it is employed; we think about the strength of the pianist; and we think about the piano itself and what a technically brilliant instrument it is.

If we are thinking about these things, are we also learning? The answer to that question depends a great deal on *how* we are thinking about *what* we are thinking. In other words, learning is influenced by how we think as well as what we think. In the case of thinking about the pianist for example, if the listener makes no connections between those things that were chosen to think about, if no relationships between posture, pedaling, instrument, and the brilliant clarity of the playing were perceived, then learning would be minimal. If, on the other hand, the listener recognized the brilliant clarity of the playing, then identified the factors that contributed to that clarity, then recognized the interdependent nature of those factors, we can be confident that learning would have taken place.

The thinking mode of learning implies an ordered process, one that links cause and effect. It begins with the recognition or identification of some thing, some phenomenon, an event, a property, perhaps a tune. The attention is captured and the thinking process is engaged. What next? Whatever is recognized is related to what is already known. The process is one of analyzing, comparing, and classifying, a process of linking the incoming information to a larger unit so that it can be rearranged and organized to benefit the learner.

In our example of the pianist, maybe the listener was thinking about how the pianist employed the sustaining pedal and recognized some features that were new to him. He may not have thought of utilizing the sustaining pedal in that particular manner and so, after careful analysis, wondered if he could try the same technique in a selection from his own repertoire. On arriving home after the concert he explored the possibilities and his thoughts were confirmed; the thinking mode had borne fruit by moving from recognition through analysis, comparison, and classification to confirmation.

> Can you recall some examples from your own experience when your learning has been patterned on the thinking mode outlined above? Imagine yourselves in the following situations and solve the problems via a thinking mode of learning: (a) you have lost your way in another city; (b) your car has stalled and refuses to start; (c) you want to know how a concerto differs from a symphony; (d) you cannot decide whether to learn to play oboe or clarinet; and (e) you have been told you sing out of tune.

You will discover as you discuss these problems that people do not think alike even though there is a general directional pattern that we all tend to follow. Our individual differences are quite marked in the thinking mode. Some of us leap across fences and miss what appear to others to be logical steps in the process. Of course we all bring different levels of understanding, prior knowledge, and experience to particular problems at any one time, so the individual differences are to be anticipated.

We can encourage learning in a thinking mode by fostering systematic and analytic inquiry about tonal properties. We can ask students to identify, relate, compare, select, explore, classify, and compile.

When we ask them to do these things, we are telling them how to think and we are suggesting an order for that thinking process.

Another example to illustrate learning via the thinking mode might have to do with a folk song, "Greensleeves" for instance. We need to consider what to think about it and how to think about it. If we are going to listen to a recorded performance of the song, we can think about any or all of the following: legato, rubato, unity, monophonic texture, clarity, conjunct melody, moderate tempo and dynamics, breathing and phrasing. We may identify these properties as we listen to the performance; they will emerge in our consciousness. As we think about the properties we will also be identifying, analyzing, comparing, and classifying. If this is a first hearing, obviously our thinking will not be well organized; it will skip about selecting here and there those things which have an immediate appeal or make an immediate impression. With repeated hearings and continued guidance we will organize our thinking more carefully. Parts will become related and linked into more meaningful wholes, and significant learning will take place. In this way the experience of music will become an *educational* experience.

In an article entitled "The Direct Teaching of Thinking as a Skill," Edward de Bono (1983) defines thinking as "the operating skill with which intelligence acts upon experience" (p. 703) and stresses that thinking skills can be taught. Activities such as those discussed above as well as guided exercises with musical problems where the "positive," "negative," and "interesting" aspects are listed can be valuable. Other exercises such as choosing music for certain purposes and analyzing the consequences of one's choices, thinking about particular excerpts and analyzing what is being thought, and developing one's own thinking strategies about music, for example, a strategy for harmonizing a melody, are all potential developers of thinking skill that can enhance musical experiences and educational experiences in general.

FEELING MODE

Our society and our schools have generally not encouraged the discussion of feelings. As a result we have frequently placed them in a category of nonverbal behaviors and ignored them. This, in spite of the fact that our actions are frequently determined by feeling as well as thinking. Our capacity to feel and to know how we feel, to discuss how we feel and why we feel that way is as vital and as important as our capacity to think, to know what we think and why we think it, and to talk about our thoughts. If we can think about something, then we can also feel it, whether it be an object like a flower or a building, an idea like "open" or "thin," or an event like a church service or a football game. If we can think about these things then we can also feel about them. And, if thinking may be defined as the operating skill with which intelligence acts upon experience, we might define feeling as the operating skill with which affective awareness, perception, and sensitivity act upon experience. Further, just as the operational skills of thinking can be enhanced via education, so may the operational skills of feeling. The more effectively feelingful we become, the greater our potential to learn via the feeling mode.

Of course we differ in the range of feelings we have and in the intensity of those feelings. Holidays, for example, make some people feel bored, others feel relaxed, some feel frustrated, while others even feel depressed. Some people feel ashamed if they are late for an appointment, while others feel nonchalant. Some people feel angry about the cost of living while others feel devastated. In this last example the feelings are similar but the intensities of the feelings are markedly different.

Some feelings are general or vague and others are quite specific. For example, a musical event may make some people feel moved while others feel a more specific response such as pride or reverence or just a sense of being refreshed. A certain event may make one person feel apprehensive; the same event for another person may produce fear; a third person may feel terror. A musical event may make one person feel relaxed; the same event for another person may produce joy; a third person may feel ecstacy. While everyone feels something, we do not all feel the same.

> Listen to a short musical excerpt in class and discuss (a) your range of feelings and (b) the intensity of your feelings. Choose your words carefully.

How do we learn via the feeling mode in music? In order to answer this question we have to realize that, like thinking, feeling can be superficial and fragmentary but that is not our goal. Feeling music can be much more than a capricious or whimsical response. It involves, as we shall see, the capacity to relate and sustain human experiences that are evoked by the tonal properties. What are these experiences?

At their most elemental level they are experiences of *imagery*. When we listen to *Peter and the Wolf* or *The Carnival of the Animals* or any other music that has an accompanying narrative, we tend to imagine the characters and events in the narrative rather than the tonal events themselves. We feel frightened by the imagery of the wolf or we feel relief as we imagine the hunters finding the duck alive in the wolf's stomach! The images become a bridge between the tonal properties and our own feelings. Such imagery may at times even substitute for the tonal properties in affecting our responses. If there is no accompanying narrative there may be a title; Debussy's *Claire de Lune* and Chopin's *Revolutionary Etude* come to mind. When we listen to these particular works in the imagery mode with titles in mind, we are likely to feel as if we were viewing moonlight or participating in uprisings, and, accordingly, we could feel serene, quiet, or lonely on the one hand and frustrated, belligerent, or aggressive on the other. In each case, the music was originally conceived as the result of physical events which in turn led to musical events. Some listeners may wish to translate the musical events back into the physical events (in their imaginations) but not all wish to do that. Some prefer to accept the composer's derivation in the *music* and let that stand as the basis for their feelings; that kind of experiencing will be explained further on in the chapter.

Other obvious examples of music that make us feel in rather general and universal ways include marches that tend to produce feelings of energy, patriotism, or loyalty and church music that produces or is intended to produce feelings of humility, worship, or serenity. These are musics composed with specific social and religious functions in mind and are therefore less ambiguous than much of the repertoire studied in schools.

Imagining events derived from narratives or titles may help us feel music, but it may also become a barrier to feeling music when narratives and titles are not available. Therefore, this way of feeling music via an image should be used discreetly. Students should not become dependent on a series of images in order to respond to music. They need to feel, to respond to the direct impact of the tonal properties. If there is no image what do we feel? At one extreme, we may feel tossed about in a flurry of unrelated feelings while, at the other, we may feel a depth and range of intensity within one principal feeling.

By way of an example, let us revisit the folk song "Greensleeves" which we thought about earlier, only this time, instead of thinking about the tonal properties of the music, let's just feel them. What do we feel? We might sense a gentle momentum; we might feel free and floating; we could feel calm and refreshed. These feelings are generated by the experience of movement within the tonal properties; they represent quite a few different facets of simply feeling good, rather than feeling anxious or feeling bored. In this example there may be a range of goodness in the sense that we have some favorite spots in the music, peak spots if you will, but there may not be depth or an intense range of feeling, given the moderate nature of the musical stimuli.

By way of comparison, how might we feel when we hear the last movement of Beethoven's *Fifth Symphony?* Here most Western persons will tend to feel tremendous energy and excitement, a sense of charging along, almost in a frenzy at times. We might feel alive, committed, and, ultimately, successful. The feelings are potentially intense, strong, and powerful. They are feelings that are known to us outside music and we feel secure whether it be in a physical or a musical environment. On the other hand, if we were to listen to some representative examples of contemporary music, we might be less likely to feel secure. We might feel excited, challenged, confused, or disturbed perhaps; we might feel overwhelmed; we might feel stretched, tense, threatened, or frightened, but secure? That is less likely. The reason is fairly obvious insofar as our contemporary society tends toward insecurity. There may be a diversity of feelings, but they probably include negative feelings that relate to anxiety, confusion, and even guilt, feelings that are far removed from seemingly gentler times and places.

When we feel music in these ways, we are responding to the tonal properties in terms of *metaphor* rather than image. The sounds evoke and suggest experiences of movement and qualities of feeling experienced at other times and in other places: echoes, amplified echoes, or clarifications of things that we have done previously or perhaps things that others have done that we would like to have been part of, recollections and clarifications of feelings rather than feelings per se.

There is another way to feel music that goes beyond the image and the metaphor to draw an *analogy with life* and the living process. When we feel music in this way, we experience the flow of life with the flow of the music. Instead of individual feeling states such as we discussed above, we now feel a continuous process analogous with life itself. We might feel growth and decay, subtle deviations, complexities and resolutions, inhibition within continuity, expansion and contraction, novelty and predictability, separateness and oneness. These feelings are not static or isolated; they represent a continuous flow of sensation, of life.

When we considered learning via the thinking mode, we realized that, for thinking to contribute to learning, it was important to relate how we think to what we think. We found that aesthetic properties needed to be related to elemental and physical properties and vice versa if learning was to be substantive. We also found that learning via thinking was an ordered process moving from recognition and analysis to confirmation and application. Is there a similar pattern in learning how to feel music?

Feeling music is experiencing it from the inside by allowing it to become part of us so that we breathe with it, move with it, hum and sing with it; in short, we identify with it. When we do this we are not outside the tonal phenomena thinking about it and analyzing it; we are inside the music adapting it as an extension of ourselves. For this to happen, we need a certain freedom and openness, a willingness to withhold judgment for the time being, an ability to allow ourselves to be directed by the life of the music. Our starting point is not analysis and comparison but, rather, sensing the flow of the music. We explore and imagine; we anticipate; we dream a little and we make discoveries; we find ourselves entering into an intimate dialogue as with a very close friend, interacting, being surprised and sometimes disappointed but always flowing with the events. It is a kind of spontaneous role-playing game in which the listener allows feelings about the music to transform him or her.

This clearly is not a thinking process; it is a state of mind or attitude in which the listener is willing to be moved by the music. The order of feeling is not linear, systematic, or sequential; it is spatial and divergent. The beginning of the feeling mode may be confused or vague imagery, with one or two stronger metaphors appearing momentarily. As the dialogue between the "metaphoric mind" and music develops, the intent becomes clearer, more details are included; the feelings intensify and the scope broadens; the mind is alert and we begin to sense relationships within larger units. The process continues until we are swept midstream into an analogy with life, feeling the hesitations, the limits, the thrusts, the parries, and the constant flow of events.

Listen to a short excerpt of music and make a note of what you feel while you are listening to the music. Are you able to distinguish among the three ways of feeling: imagery, metaphor, and life analogy? How similar are the feelings experienced by the class? Discuss and share your feelings about the music; then listen to it again. Has sharing increased the range and/or intensity of your feelings?

SHARING MODE

The thinking mode of learning focused on tonal properties; the feeling mode of learning focused on human experiences; what then is the focus of the sharing mode of learning? The same questions arise here as in thinking and feeling modes, namely what is shared and how do we share? In attempting to answer these questions, we shall find a focus for the sharing mode of learning. But, first, let us extend our analogous definitions one step further to speculate that musical sharing might be defined as the operating skill with which one's personal and social natures act on musical experiences. Again, such operating skills can be enhanced through analysis and guided exercises, through education which in turn enhances our potential to learn via the sharing mode.

Figure 8 is a simplified representation of the relationships among thinking, feeling, and sharing. The starting point for any learning mode in music education is hearing music, either physically or in our imaginations. The sounds are then processed via thinking and/or feeling, both of which are internal interactive operations. In these learning modes, input comes from sounds and from self, and ideally is drawn together in the mind. Sharing, on the other hand, is an external interactive operation; it represents an "outing" of what is thought and felt, and as such it provides for valuable feedback. So the focus for the sharing mode is a blend of thought and feelings about music. Sometimes the blend may be somewhat one-sided in the sense that thought may dominate, or vice versa, but generally the presumed ideal is a balance between these two modes, a balance that results in mutual enhancement of the holistic life-process.

> Listen to a movement from a sonata or symphony or any similar type of composition and share your thoughts about the tonal properties heard and identified in the work. You will employ a professional vocabulary to describe the properties; then share your feelings about the work utilizing an experiential vocabulary drawn from those categories in the feeling mode of learning. If you find it easier to share via thoughts rather than feelings, or the reverse, ask yourself if this is indicative of your general behavior. Finally, can you write a statement about the recording employing both professional and experiential vocabularies which you are then willing to share with the class? In this way you will move towards a balance between the two modes of learning.

When we share music via language it is very easy to employ words without careful selection or judgment. If we select our vocabulary with care we can become more sensitive to the tonal properties we

Figure 8   Fundamental Music Learning Modes and Their Basic Relationships

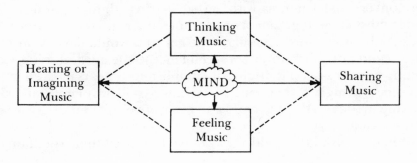

hear and to our own range and depth of feeling. For example, a particular melody may be described by one person simply as being a "happy tune," while another person may say, "This melody has a gentle contour but there are also some lively, syncopated, rhythmic jolts." Obviously we learn more about the properties of the melody and the qualities of the human response in the second statement than in the first.

The sharing mode of learning via discussion provides excellent opportunities to draw thoughts and feelings together for mutual enhancement where they might otherwise remain separate or in an elementary stage of development. Take for example a feeling of excitement which in itself is a very generalized response, but is commonly felt as part of a musical experience. If the response is limited to excitement, that is, if there is no thinking response and if the excitement is not related to human experiences, for example, experiences of growth or surprise (which might result from crescendos, dynamic outbursts or tonal contrasts), then the musical experience is unlikely to be educational. When thoughts and feelings about this particular example are shared, the general feeling of excitement is likely to be more precisely focused and refined and it is likely to be related to the tonal properties that caused the response. Consequently, perception will increase, the range of possible responses will expand, and the quality of the response will tend to heighten.

Another example might have to do with a person whose response is limited to thinking rather than feeling music. This time let us assume the response is couched in terms of identifying repeated rhythmic patterns. Repetition at one extreme may generate feelings of boredom, and, at the other, feelings of tension or frustration. By recognizing and sharing the range of *possible* feelings, we are likely to increase the range of *actual* feelings. The repeated patterns may then produce boredom or frustration, but also a range of more specific and potentially meaningful feelings such as anxiety, anger, hope, or anticipation.

If we are not sharing verbally then we may share nonverbally through gesture, performance, composition, or listening. For effective nonverbal sharing, as with verbal sharing, thinking and feeling modes must come together. For example, if a conductor shared only feelings about the music, it is likely the gestures would have a confused pattern and possibly bear little resemblance to the musical score. Conducting gestures need thought, discipline, and rehearsal. Even more, they need a high component of technical skill involving analytical thinking modes on the one hand and innovative and expressive modes on the other.

When we ask little children to move to music, their spontaneous gestures are more closely aligned to feeling than to thinking. Beginning conductors often are at the opposite extreme. Their thoughts are so totally committed to maintaining a clear pattern that there is little or no scope for expressive human qualities. The ideal is, of course, a blend of both modes in which a conductor shares deep and profound feelings through a technique that represents careful and logical thinking.

> As a fun exercise in your class, you may like to select one short orchestral excerpt and have everyone conduct an imaginary orchestra. Alternate feeling and thinking emphases and then try to blend the two modes into a balanced sharing mode.

When it comes to the area of nonverbal sharing via performance, we have all experienced occasions where feeling dominates or thinking dominates. A feeling performance is characterized by personal overindulgence on the part of the performer. Concern for stylistic traditions and aesthetic subtleties is absent. Instead there is a living out of unstructured emotionalism that is essentially alien to the art of music. Conversely, performances are sometimes over-analyzed and over-practiced and they create an impersonal, sterile response in which athletics seem to win out over aesthetics. A performance that is genuinely musical is neither athletic nor anaesthetic. The epitome of an aesthetic performance is the coming together of thought and feeling within subtle parameters relating to musical style and cultural context.

It is sometimes argued that skills and expressiveness are to be separated in performance development. We may say, "Get the notes right first and then add the expression." The danger in so doing is that we accentuate the differences between thought and feeling, sometimes to such an extent that they never come together to make a convincing musical whole (see Haack, 1982). The sharing mode of learning fosters thought and feeling at all stages of growth based on the premise that one area assists the other in terms of self-knowledge as well as its corollary, musical insight.

> You probably all have performing ability on at least one musical instrument. Choose a short composition that you wish to share with the class; perform it and discuss your performance in terms of what was shared. Did you achieve a balance between thinking and feeling modes? How much of yourself did you reveal? Did your evaluation of the performance coincide with your colleagues'? If there is time, repeat the performance and the evaluation.

Learning via the sharing mode can be facilitated if we and our students make more use of and are less self-conscious about syllabizing. Frequently our feelings can be sharpened and refined by exploring performing possibilities in our minds or by humming or employing neutral, verbally meaningless syllables in rehearsal and practice situations. The advantage of this procedure is that it encourages and supports musical imagination, thought, and feeling, particularly where performance skill is limited. Syllabizing helps to clarify musical intent and allows musical ideas to be shared in direct and educationally stimulating ways. To illustrate the point:

Select a well known song and see how many ways it can be syllabized in your class. Could it be sung in as many ways? Evaluate your own vocabulary of syllables in terms of range and precision.

Another form of learning via the sharing mode involves composition, improvisation, and arranging. Shaping a series of musical events spontaneously or over a period of time involves thinking and feeling processes. It involves a willingness to share human experiences through tonal properties. Great composers begin with a profound awareness of human experience which is in turn projected through tonal properties in ways that can make us feel moved. In other words, composing involves a good deal more than playing with sounds; it is the quality of the sounds and the ways in which they can be combined to produce analogies with life that make composing so challenging, so rewarding, and so beneficial to mankind. (See the final suggestion in the "Extensions" section of this chapter.)

In the sharing mode of learning we utilize verbal and nonverbal behaviors. We interact directly or indirectly with other persons, learning how they think and feel about music, accepting those things that are valuable for our own growth and leaving those that seem offensive or irrelevant. We freely offer our own discoveries for what they may be worth to others.

MEANINGS AND VALUES

We need to keep before us constantly the fact that music becomes educationally significant only when it contributes to human development, that is, when learning takes place. We define learning here as a process of deriving meaning from experiences where meaning represents the interaction, the marriage of thinking and feeling. In music education learning takes place when a musical experience has meaning for a student; that is, when one's own thoughts and feelings are related to a musical event (Tait, 1981, p. 122.)

At the beginning of this chapter we asked the question: What is it that we want our students to learn in music classes? We could rephrase the question by asking: What meanings and values can be derived from learning music? Before attempting to answer these questions, perhaps you might have a brief discussion with your colleagues to try to decide what meanings you usually derive from your musical experiences. Can you pinpoint some of the values you have derived from music?

Clearly the most important point to remember is that the range of possible meanings of music or even of a single composition is vast and variable. From a particular musical event, no single "right" meaning is to be derived but rather a whole series of meanings. On the one hand, we may learn about the elements of music, the forms of music, how sounds are produced, and the kinds of aesthetic properties that emerge when elements are arranged in certain ways. On the other hand, we can learn how to feel music through imagery, by means of metaphoric derivation, or by drawing analogies with the living process. In order to help clarify the vast range of potential learnings available through music, we suggest that you use the sample checklist provided here as figure 9 or devise a more comprehensive checklist of your own.

If we are interested not only in a range of meanings but in the quality of those meanings, then we must be concerned with how meanings are acquired. In other words, quality of meaning is directly related to quality of learning. We have attempted to show the nature of musical meaning to be unique in the sense that it is dependent on both tonal properties and human experiences. Further, the qualitative meaning extends from simple to complex potential in both areas. For example, if the connections made are limited to physical properties (tonal) and imagined experiences (human), the qualitative meanings will be relatively simple and unsophisticated. If, on the other hand, relatedness develops at the level of aesthetic properties and life analog, then the qualitative meanings will be complex and possibly quite profound.

Many other possibilities exist for deriving musical meaning depending on the kinds of linkage or the kinds of units of relatedness that develop in the mind of the musical consumer or producer. It may help to visualize this by reconsidering the model of a synthesis of tonal and human phenomena presented as figure 2 in chapter 2.

The maximum potential for meaning is realized when all musical properties are interacting with all human experiences by means of thinking, feeling, and sharing modes of learning. This may seem impossibly complicated but in fact it helps to explain why people keep coming back to one composition time and again throughout their lives and derive new meanings because new links are forged within the interactive processes. Obviously if musical experience is limited to one learning mode, thinking, for example, then qualitative mean-

Figure 9 Musical Learning Self-Evaluation Checklist

A. When I am involved with music,
    I PERCEIVE:

melody

harmony

rhythm

texture

dynamics

phrasing

instruments

tonality

timbre

patterns

line

growth

contrast

style

form

(and other "professional" terms)

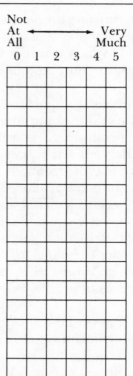

B. When I am involved with music,
    I EXPERIENCE:

images

shapes

movement

dramatic events

boredom

confusion

frustration

serenity

nature

fulfillment

wholeness

environmental change

tension

resolution

(and other "experiential" terms)

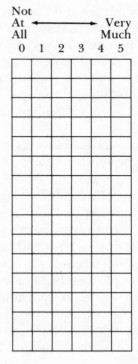

Figure 9 *(Continued)*

C. When I am involved with music,* I AM:	Not At All 0	← 1	2	→ 3	Very Much 4	5
thinking						
analyzing						
classifying						
recognizing						
distinguishing						
organizing						
combining						
listening						
observing						
feeling						
imagining						
reflecting						
exploring						
responding						
sensing						
dreaming						
imitating						
creating						
valuing						
evaluating						
(and other "behavioral" terms)						

Note: The same or similar lists can be used to analyze more specific involvement emphases, e.g., "When I compose music," "When I perform music," or "When I listen to music."

ing is also limited. It is no mean feat to juggle the components of a musical event, drawing on our memories, projecting in our imaginations, investing our feelings, and analyzing our thoughts, and all of this from moment to moment as the musical work unfolds.

> Do the kinds of meanings you most frequently derive from your musical experiences vary with the repertoire you happen to be working on?

The connection between meaning and value is rather clear in that a person who derives a range and depth of musical meaning from a musical experience is likely to value that experience. In other words, meaning and value parallel one another. We value those things that have most meaning for us: our closest friends, our personal possessions, our vacation spots, our pets, and so forth. We value them because they mean so much to us. The key to value is meaning. A person who does not value music probably derives very little meaning from it; the range and quality of meaning are most likely limited and shallow. Conversely, one who does value music has found it meaningful and useful; and here, in a few words, is the key to the concern of motivation.

If, as a result of musical experiences, persons are able to increase self-knowledge and are able to interact more effectively internally and socially, then it is more than likely they will value music, and themselves, more highly. Thus musical learning is viewed as an integrating and broadening experience with a high yield potential for meaning and value. Learning music should have, as its ultimate goal, development of the ability to use and interact with music wisely, for personal and social growth, for the fulfillment of one's own needs and those of others.

EXTENSIONS

Statements

1. "The only man who is educated is the man who has learned how to learn; the man who has learned how to adapt and change; the man who has realized that no knowledge is secure, that only the process of seeking knowledge gives a basis for security." Rogers, Carl R., *Freedom to Learn* (Columbus, Ohio: Charles Merrill Publishing Co., 1969), p. 104.
2. "The construction of knowledge, as distinct from the attainment of it, presumes freedom and skill in sharing and use of controlled emotion and imagery. We say then that the children are involved, are making the lessons their own, are aroused, excited, interested, original, inventive and so on." Jones, Richard M., *Fantasy and Feeling in Education* (London: University of London Press, 1968), p. 26.
3. "Changing the child's behavior without changing his perceptions is unlikely to produce any permanent variation in his behavior. On the other hand, changes in his perception must almost certainly result in some different kind of action." Combs, Arthur W., *Educational Accountability: Beyond Behavioral Objectives* (Washington: Association for Supervision and Curriculum Development, 1972), p. 19.
4. "This capacity to build coordinating schemas, to make multiple descriptions of the 'same' phenomena is, I think, a basic skill, perhaps *the* basic skill in learning how to learn—and that ultimately means learning how to learn something: Math skills, language skills, and all the rest." Bamburger, Jeanne, "Intuitive and Formal Musical Knowledge," in *The Arts,*

Cognition and Basic Skills, ed. Stanley S. Madeja (St. Louis: CEMREL, 1978), p. 203.

5. "Grasping the structure of a subject is understanding it in a way that permits many other things to be related to it meaningfully. To learn structure in short is to learn how things are related." Bruner, Jerome S., *The Process of Education* (Cambridge: Harvard University Press, 1961), p. 7.

Questions and Suggestions

1. What were the sources of your musical motivation? How have they changed? How would you assess your students' motivation?
2. Give examples of the kinds of extrinsic and intrinsic motivation you would expect to find in a school music program.
3. How has your understanding of musicality changed? What have you learned about your own musicality at this time? Do you see motivation and imagination as being related?
4. Describe how you would approach motivation in a junior high school music program. Explain your attitude towards motivation and give some examples of the steps you would take to gain maximum effectiveness.
5. What aspects of musical learning are most neglected or least successful, in your opinion? Give some specific examples of how you would propose to improve the situation.
6. How do memory and imagination serve a learning function in your musical life?
7. What is meant by the phrase "learning by feeling"?
8. Discuss some of the ways in which musical learnings may differ from other areas in the high school curriculum. How are you going to accommodate these unique musical learnings in your program?
9. If the musical imagination is even more important than the musical ear, how can you nourish the musical imagination?
10. Has your own music education involved more doing than learning? If you were given similar opportunities again, what changes would you wish to make? Why?
11. We all learn according to the kinds of people we are. What are some of the ways you intend to implement this principle in your classroom or studio?
12. If music education is both teaching and learning music, in what ways are these two processes related?
13. What makes for readiness in learning music? How does readiness manifest itself in a learning situation?
14. Discuss the role of imitation in learning music. Is it more appropriate at one stage of learning than another, or in one area of the curriculum than another? Can imitation and imagination support one another in learning music? Give examples.
15. Reflect on how you learn a piece of music. Has your approach to learning music changed over the years? In what ways? Would you describe your approach as emphasizing systematic and sequential or intuitive and creative processes, or does it possess elements of both?

16. The ability to discriminate tonal qualities is a fundamental part of the musical experience. Which tonal qualities can you discriminate most easily and which are most difficult for you? Has this always been so and what are you doing to gain a better balance?

17. The following words indicate some of the things we do when we learn: talk, explore, try, organize, conceptualize, extend, watch, discover, react, feel, analyze, identify, reject, accept, respond, compare, create, relate, and imagine. Which of these words or any other of your choice most accurately describe your process of learning a new piece of music? Could you arrange the words to indicate a sequence in the process, and to what extent is that sequence typical of all your musical learning, or, for that matter, all your learning?

18. When next you embark on a specific musical learning task, make a conscious effort to increase the frequency of one aspect of the thinking mode. It might be comparison, or analysis, or repetition, or extension, but experiment in this fashion and evaluate the results.

19. Can we honestly evaluate students' musical values and artistic tastes if we teach them what to think rather than how to think?

20. When next you are engaged in a musical experience such as performing or listening, make a conscious effort to link disparate phenomena, events that you have not tried to relate previously. For example, attempt to link rhythmic pattern and harmonic density, or melodic contour and articulation, or tonal nuance and tessitura. If you can begin to build relationships between such perceptions, then learning will become more effective.

21. Can you think of a teacher who involved your feelings in the learning process? How was it handled? Were the results positive or negative? Could the results have been different if the strategy had been different?

22. List those aspects of music you most frequently think about. Now, what do you *feel* about them?

23. Is your feeling about music limited to fleeting imagery or capricious whimsy of some kind? Do you get swept away in an emotional wave? Can you describe the range and intensity of your feelings for music?

24. When we feel music as an extension of ourselves, we are learning about ourselves as well as about music. How can we deal with this profound aspect of music education more adequately in the classroom and studio?

25. When you have recognized your feelings as being involved in the learning process, what have you done? Have you ignored them, or have you acknowledged them and related them to the goals and tasks at hand? Has your response differed depending on musical and nonmusical subjects or positive or negative feelings?

26. If a teacher encourages thinking by questioning and challenging, how can a teacher encourage feeling? And what about sharing?

27. Can you remember when you first began experiencing music as both tonal and human phenomena? What precipitated your awareness of this linkage? Had you always experienced music in this way?

28. What is the relationship between sharing and competing? Are they op-

posites or parts of one another? Certain sharing aspects of music education seem, like life itself, to involve a notable amount of competitive activity. Considering the ideas in part I as well as the present chapter, to what extent do you believe such traditions as chair competition and music contests to be educationally useful or abuseful?

29. Reflect on your music learning via sharing. Are you more comfortable sharing thoughts and ideas than feelings in music, or vice versa? Why should music teaching involve both aspects of sharing?

30. Can too much sharing or inappropriate sharing inhibit curiosity, creativity, exploration, and discovery? Give examples.

31. If meaning represents the successful marriage of thinking and feeling, how can we increase musical meaning in music education? Plan some specific experiences that will illustrate what you have in mind.

32. Discuss musical values with your colleagues. Try to determine if their musical values are an outgrowth of personal meanings based on experiences with music. What are the implications for values education in music?

33. Things that are meaningful are useful and need-fulfilling and these are prime factors in valuing. Therefore, what are some ways in which we can enhance our students' awareness of values and their qualitative experiences with music? That is, how can we help students increase their awareness of the broad range of functions that music may serve; and how can we help them increase their understanding and ability to choose music that is most appropriate and effective for the circumstances in which they use it?

34. Try to share some of your human insight and tonal understanding by improvising or composing some short, contrasting musical events. Your source of derivation may be an image, a metaphor, or an analog of the living process. Select the musical properties you want, the sound sources, and the sequence, and devise a notational scheme if necessary. Perform for others and have them assist you in evaluating: To what extent did you share what you intended to share?

REFERENCES AND READINGS

Ausubel, David P. *The Psychology of Meaningful Verbal Learning and Retention*. New York: Grune and Stratton, 1963.

Bruner, Jerome S. *The Process of Education*. New York: Random House/Vintage Books, 1963.

de Bono, Edward. "The Direct Teaching of Thinking as a Skill." *Phi Delta Kappan*, June 1983, pp. 703–08.

Gagne, Robert M. *The Conditions of Learning*. New York: Holt, Rinehart and Winston, 1965.

Gardner, Howard. *The Arts and Human Development*. New York: John Wiley, 1973.

Gates, A., and Bradshaw, J.L. "The Role of the Cerebral Hemisphere in Music." *Brain and Language*, 1977, vol. 4, pp. 403–31.

Haack, Paul. "Paint-by-Numbers Music." *Music Educators Journal*, May 1982, pp. 35–36.

Hunt, James M. *Intelligence and Experience.* New York: Ronald Press, 1961.

Madeja, Stanley S. *The Arts, Cognition, and Basic Skills.* St. Louis: CEMREL, 1978.

Mager, Robert F. *Developing Attitude Toward Learning.* Palo Alto, Calif.: Fearon Publishers, 1968.

Mursell, James L. "Growth Processes in Music Education." In *Basic Concepts in Music Education.* Chicago: National Society for the Study of Education, 57th Yearbook, 1958.

National Association of Secondary School Principals (NASSP). *Student Learning Styles: Diagnosing and Prescribing Programs.* Reston, Va.: NASSP, 1979.

Peters, David G., and Miller, Robert F. *Music Teaching and Learning.* New York: Longmans, 1982.

Piaget, Jean. *The Language and Thought of the Child.* Cleveland: World Publishing Co., 1965.

Rogers, Carl. *Freedom to Learn.* Columbus, Ohio: Charles Merrill, 1969.

Rogers, Carl. "Toward a Theory of Creativity." In *Creativity and its Cultivation,* edited by N.H. Anderson. New York: Harper and Row, 1959.

Silver, M. *Values Education.* Washington: National Education Association, 1976.

Tait, Malcolm. "Motivation and Affect." In *Documentary Report of the Ann Arbor Symposium: Applications of Psychology to the Teaching and Learning of Music.* Reston, Va.: Music Educators National Conference, 1981.

Thorpe, Louis P. "Learning Theory and Music Teaching." In *Basic Concepts in Music Education.* Chicago: National Society for the Study of Education, 57th Yearbook, 1958.

6

Planning

Underlying Concepts: The beginnings of planning lie in human needs and the nature of the educational experiences that are envisaged to meet those needs. The nature of these experiences determines the nature of the musical program and the nature of the program determines the characteristic qualities of those who graduate from it.

Planning is a multidimensional activity that will be most effective when all concerned are involved in the process.

Planning needs to embrace the three basic variables of the profession, namely: music, teachers, and students. When the dynamic interaction between these variables is understood and articulated, then planning is most likely to be effective.

The function of planning is to make the musical experience educational and the educational experience musical. In order for that to happen, three interacting vocabularies are needed: (a) a vocabulary to describe the properties of tonal phenomena, (b) a vocabulary to describe the nature of human experience, and (c) a vocabulary to describe educational behaviors that link tonal properties to human experience.

Why do we need to plan? Some teachers view planning as a tedious responsibility with little practical impact on the quality of teaching or learning. Other teachers spend weeks planning their music curriculum and produce sizable documents in the process. Teacher education also has varied enormously in the amount of time devoted to planning. Some students are expected to prepare little more than half a dozen lesson plans while others spend several weeks dealing with all kinds of goals and objectives, classroom activities, and educational procedures.

A brief examination of our professional literature indicates that many people have written extensively on the importance of planning for teaching but the writing varies in terms of its rhetoric and thrust. Sometimes it is quite general and focuses on broadly based social or educational goals while at other times it is highly specific, attempting to determine not only what should take place in the classroom, but also how it should take place, when, and what the results will be.

Perhaps the most difficult problem facing the teacher concerned with planning is to translate beliefs about the nature and function of music into daily lessons. Music itself may be nonliteral but when we plan we have to use words and this immediately has the effect of limiting the scope of the subject. Planning tends to emphasize those aspects of music that can be easily named, that can be readily identified, but it generally tends to de-emphasize the more intangible qualities which probably lie at the heart of music for most of us. This is particularly true if we limit our vocabulary to that traditionally employed in planning for music teaching, but it need not be so. We will consider this further on in the chapter. At this point, suffice it to say that it is vitally important to bear in mind as we plan that we are going to have to add other dimensions to our students' musical experiences as we teach. Those "intangibles" may not be present on paper in the planning process but they certainly need to be present in the teaching and learning process if we are going to do justice to our subject and our students.

As we attempt to bridge the gap between our beliefs about music and our daily lessons, we will introduce four levels of planning, moving from broadly based philosophical considerations, through aims and objectives, to quite specific kinds of classroom experiences. As we do so it is essential to keep in mind the fact that planning is indeed a multidimensional activity, and one that will be most effective when all concerned are involved appropriately in the process. Generally, this means that in planning at the philosophical principles level or dimension, more of the concerned groups, parents, administrators, and other faculty will have more input; while at the other end of the process, at the actual daily experience level, individual teachers and their students' ideas will be predominant. Figure 10 provides a graphic overview of the various planning levels along with examples of statements associated with each of the levels.

Reflect on your own music education. To what extent were you familiar with the kinds of planning that went into it? Did you help to determine the goals for any programs? Were you aware of your teachers' long- or short-term goals? How might all this relate to student motivation?

Figure 10 An Overview of Planning Levels for Music Education

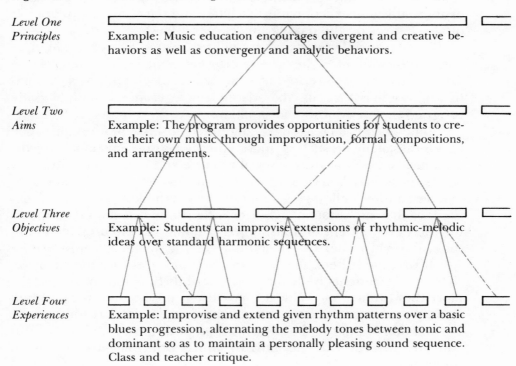

Level One
Principles

Example: Music education encourages divergent and creative behaviors as well as convergent and analytic behaviors.

Level Two
Aims

Example: The program provides opportunities for students to create their own music through improvisation, formal compositions,
and arrangements.

Level Three
Objectives

Example: Students can improvise extensions of rhythmic-melodic
ideas over standard harmonic sequences.

Level Four
Experiences

Example: Improvise and extend given rhythm patterns over a basic
blues progression, alternating the melody tones between tonic and
dominant so as to maintain a personally pleasing sound sequence.
Class and teacher critique.

LEVEL ONE PLANNING: PRINCIPLES

The most general order or category of planning is a statement of
principles that represent a teacher's philosophy of music education.
According to Leonhard and House (1972), "Principles may be regarded as fundamental truths upon which one may chart his actions"
(p. 40). Such principles may emphasize students, music, or teaching
because together these facts represent the cornerstones of music education. When we state our principles we are not yet thinking about
specific programs but rather we are concerned with statements of
belief about the nature of music education. For example, Schwadron
(1966) states a principle when he says, "Music education functions
most effectively when both intellectual and emotional factors are considered coordinates in the development of aesthetic perception" (p.
93). Carl Rogers (1969) states a principle when he writes: "Significant
learning takes place when the subject matter is perceived by the student as having relevance for his own purposes" (p. 158). This principle
relates to the learning process more than to the subject but it is clearly
relevant to music education. Similarly, the following statement by
Bruner (1966) can be considered a principle that relates to teaching:

"Since learning and problem solving depend upon the exploration of alternatives, instruction must facilitate and regulate the exploration of alternatives on the part of the learner" (p. 43).

These principles as stated are not yet related to a program or to a group of students. They are in effect statements of belief held by individuals and they represent summations of philosophies or parts of philosophies that may be adapted by a teacher to virtually any program or any educational situation.

Sometimes principles have amounted to little more than vague rhetorical statements such as "music education assists emotional growth" or "music education fosters social reliance and individual initiative." While there may be elements of truth in such statements, they tend to have a rather hollow ring about them. This hollowness results from the fact that such statements offer little if any direction or impetus for the development of aims, objectives, and experiences for life in the real-world school. Contrast them with the statements of principles which preceded them. Those principles, and this one for example, "The more students understand the various functions of music, the more they can use and value it," have direct implications for program content and methodology. Effective principles lead readily to the formulation of philosophically consistent program aims. They inform and give direction to the aims by which principles are related to programs.

Why is it important for planning to grow naturally and consistently from a basic philosophy?

LEVEL TWO PLANNING: AIMS

So, the second level of planning relates principles to the aims of a particular program, be it a high school choral program, an elementary classroom program, or a college degree program. In stating aims, we have in mind general outcomes for a program that are congruent with stated principles and philosophies. When we develop a list of aims for a program, we are thinking also about a group of students whose needs are to be served by that program. That does not mean that we forget about philosophies and principles, but rather that they will provide the bases for and find their practical applications in the aims of a particular student-oriented program. For example, we might consider the following aims as representing long-range expectations for an undergraduate college program in music education. The program will develop in music education majors the ability to:

1. Be articulate about the general nature of music and the ways in which it may be related to education.

2. Discuss and demonstrate the ways in which music functions in the daily lives of students.

3. Be receptive to a variety of aesthetic meanings and be capable of discussing them in relation to a variety of musics.

4. Possess a comprehensive understanding of musical elements and forms.

5. Relate musical elements and forms to historical, stylistic, and geographic frames.

6. Demonstrate the understanding in 4 and 5 above (a) through an individual performing media of their choice, and (b) in a small and large ensemble setting.

7. Improvise and arrange in ways that can be applied to teaching situations.

8. Demonstrate creative and flexible attitudes in their teaching.

9. Show spontaneous and genuine interest in the welfare and progress of their students.

10. Identify valuable learning materials and strategies and utilize them in valid learning experiences.

> Make some enquiries about the aims of the program you are in, or about some of the programs you visit in elementary or secondary schools. The aims may be implicit rather than explicit, but, in any event, try to determine what person or group of persons is responsible for the determination of those aims.

Aims are helpful in providing a bird's-eye view of the intent of a program. They help pull together individual philosophies into a coherent whole and provide a focus of action. A statement of aims is an essential component of any program, for without it there can be little sense of direction and no basis for evaluating progress or growth. Nevertheless, statements of aims by their nature and purpose are not sufficiently specific to provide clear guidelines for student behaviors, and therefore a third level of planning is essential.

LEVEL THREE PLANNING: OBJECTIVES

Objectives help to clarify the student behaviors that should occur within a program. You will realize that with each successive breakdown in the planning process, the quantity of planning statements increases and the quality of specificity also increases. We may start out with only five or ten principles but these may generate as many as thirty or more aims. Because objectives relate quite specifically to student behaviors, their potential number increases dramatically. A teacher may generate scores of objectives for students in one particular program. For example, consider two aims for a junior high school general music program. There would of course be several aims for the total program, and several objectives for each aim, but we will consider here just two aims and several objectives for each.

AIM: THE PROGRAM WILL ENCOURAGE STUDENTS TO SELECT AND LEARN TO PLAY A SIMPLE INSTRUMENT OF THEIR CHOICE WITH FLUENCY AND IN A MUSICALLY EXPRESSIVE MANNER.

Objectives

1. Identify, describe, and give reactions to a variety of simple musical instruments; select and give reasons for selection.
2. Explore sound production on those instruments (expressive range, techniques of production); listen to performances on the selected instruments; and discuss the expressive qualities projected in the performances.
3. Improvise or compose short musical statements which demonstrate a wide range of personal ideas and feelings.
4. Devise and record a longer musical statement which incorporates contrasting ideas and feelings. Use tape cassettes, standard notation, or a personal mode of notation.
5. Select and practice exercises to develop technical fluency.
6. Read and play simple musical scores on the selected instrument.
7. Share musical insights and performing skills in small and large group settings. Analyze and discuss the performances.

AIM: ENCOURAGE THE RECOGNITION OF EXPRESSIVE AND AESTHETIC QUALITIES WITHIN THE STUDENTS THEMSELVES BY HELPING THEM RELATE TO THOSE QUALITIES THAT THEY PERCEIVE IN THE MUSIC.

Objectives

1. Explore and discuss examples of man as a being of feeling (general, nonmusical).
2. Identify, analyze, and describe personal experiences related to or derived from artistic sources.
3. Examine recorded examples of how music functions in the lives of people (music as a part of worship, ceremony, leisure, marketing, politics, dance, military events, and so forth).
4. Recall and describe a musical experience of personal significance.
5. Recognize and identify basic musical elements and components, and consider their implications for expressive usage.
6. Experiment individually and in small groups (using tape cassettes) to communicate nonverbal expressions through sound imagery and patterns.

Some teachers have questioned the extent to which student musical behaviors can or should be preplanned. They argue that excessive specificity in planning objectives can lead to subject fragmentation and a tendency to ignore musical behaviors that are not readily observable. It is true there have been times in the drive for accountability and increasingly specific objectives when the process has seemed more of an academic exercise than a musical and educational one. Nevertheless, the need for more effective planning is recognized by most teachers.

During the 1960s and 1970s, there was a desire on the part of many educators to reinterpret the nature of music for curricular purposes; a desire to give music a more comprehensive character by spelling out a conceptual framework and by making that the central focus for study. Many practices, methods, and materials continue to reflect this emphasis today. The concepts or elements of tone, rhythm, melody, harmony, texture, and tonality were generally considered to be the raw materials of traditional Western music and, as such, provided a convenient framework for developing more specific objectives for music education. Thus, opportunities were provided for students to interact with the elements, forms, and styles of music in a variety of musicianly ways such as composing, performing, and listening.

As an example of this process, let us suppose rhythm is part of the conceptual frame introduced to a first grade class. In its simplest form, rhythm might be experienced as pulse and accent, so planning would involve selecting activities for identifying pulse and recognizing how pulse might be grouped according to accent. An obvious activity would include clapping, perhaps echo clapping, clapping with a recording, with a song, or with a chant or poem. Children might compose a chant based on the pulse and accents as they occur in their own names. As the children became experienced and confident with pulse and accent, other rhythmic subcomponents might be introduced, and so the spiral would develop.

With further schooling, rhythm becomes an element that takes on broader and deeper significance as students experience tempo changes, the introduction of rubato, syncopation, multimeter, and augmentation and diminution. In addition, this perceptual-conceptual broadening is experienced in varying historic, geographic, and stylistic frames. Augmentation may be related to fugal form and baroque texture, while polyrhythm can be viewed as a sophisticated characteristic of many African musics. It is assumed that progressing students will internally relate increased perception to increased response, so that knowledge of and experience with rubato, for example, will increase the intensity and subtlety of the rhythmic response.

Additional concepts and subconcepts can be added according to

Figure 11 Examples of Cyclical Development of Musical Concepts

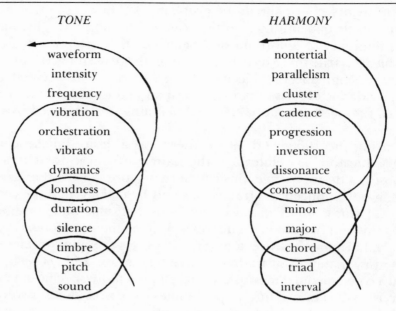

the level of sophistication and competence that is desired, and also according to the ways in which knowledge of the musical art develops. Figure 11 expands on the preceding example of rhythm by graphically presenting examples of the cyclical development of concepts concerned with tone and harmony.

Underlying this approach has been the assumption of a developmental way of knowing music, a way that parallels human development itself. This is probably true in a broad sense, but it is certainly not proven in matters of detail. We cannot say, for example, that study of duration should follow or precede meter, and indeed even the age-old problem of the primacy of rhythm or melody is still an unresolved "chicken or egg" controversy. Nevertheless, the idea of structuring the elements of music in a developmental flow has appealed to many music educators. Numerous school systems have adopted the approach and this has led to an increase in the cognitive and perceptual content of music teaching.

Here is an example of Level Three Objectives planning for a conceptual emphasis. The program we have in mind is a high school choral program and the objectives are stated for the primary concept tone, and for the subconcepts of vibrato and timbre. Students will be expected to:

1. Recognize and evaluate the use of vibrato in vocal and choral performances.
2. Sing individual tones with and without vibrato.

3. Locate, discuss, and evaluate examples of vocal literature vis-à-vis appropriate vibrato techniques.
4. Intensify and relax vibrato according to stylistic demands.
5. Compile a series of recorded excerpts to illustrate a variety of vocal timbres.
6. Analyze and describe different examples of vocal timbre.
7. Explore the potential range of timbres in their own voices.
8. Match tones of varying vocal timbre.
9. Select the qualities of timbre most suited to the stylistic characteristics of particular pieces of music.
10. Relate vocal timbre to vowel production.
11. Assess the expressive or aesthetic impact of varying vocal and choral timbres.

Sometimes Level Three Objectives planning has been divorced from principles and aims. This divorcement has led to a rather isolated or independent unit approach. This kind of "topical" planning favors units or groups of activities based on themes, topics, or selected repertoire. It is a kind of sampling approach in which cyclic and progressive development is not impossible, but is difficult to achieve and tends to occur only casually if at all. The rationale for such planning is to attempt to give students something they like, something that is timely or relevant to them. Topics might include singing for fun, electronic music, youth music, music and microcomputers, music in other cultures, playing the guitar, learning to read music, music and other arts, humor in music, instruments of the orchestra, music for television, creative music, and so forth. All are worthy concerns, but often there is no central core or clear progression of content depth with these kinds of specialties. Each topic is relatively self-contained with only casual links to other topics. Similarly, in performing groups, repertoire tends to be selected primarily for immediate appeal or immediate program needs rather than for sequential learning goals requiring music of specific stylistic, aesthetic, or other functional significance. The danger of this planning, or lack thereof, is superficiality or tokenism. The interests of the students may be captured but if those interests are not challenged and related to long-term aims and principles, there is likely to be a classroom atmosphere of simple entertainment rather than education. And while entertainment has value, music has many additional values more demanding of the education process.

> Why might a predominant concern with one level of planning, such as objectives, inhibit educational progress?

There is a general danger in Level Three Objectives planning that the specifics of music may tend to dominate the educational enterprise. Critics have argued that emphasis on objectives may have increased the cognitive-conceptual component in music education, but it has often ignored the expressive-affective areas. Many of our responses to music are subjective covert behaviors, and yet we have not been very successful in finding ways to nourish such behaviors with effective planning. Rather, we have concentrated on those elements of music that can be readily identified and perceived in the hope that increased perception will engender increased response. Nevertheless, there is a profound belief within the music education profession that enhanced aesthetic response is one of the most fundamental benefits to accrue from music education, and therefore methodologies for improving that response are urgently needed. Some teachers have attempted to meet this need by utilizing Level Three Objectives planning in association with questioning techniques aimed at drawing out student responses. Examples of this kind of approach follow:

1. Select the one word from the following list that comes nearest to your concept of the ideal tone for this composition: heavy, light, hollow, rich, bell-like, warm, resonant.
2. Which of the following elements is most responsible for generating the rhythmic tension of this song: pulse, variable tempo, accent, syncopation, or polyrhythm?
3. How much flexibility do you have for tastefully varying the expressive elements in a performance of this song? Consider tempo and dynamics, for example, and explore the possibilities as you rehearse each phrase.
4. You will probably respond to the qualities of praise and jubilant celebration conveyed in this music. Explain how the composer has selected and arranged the musical elements in order to arouse those feelings.

Clearly these questions represent a genuine desire to move beyond the mere perception of tonal phenomena; but they have the disadvantage of resulting in a rather lengthy and cumbersome planning procedure, and the range of implied student behaviors is still somewhat limited.

Locate some references that discuss planning for overt and covert musical behaviors. List the pros and cons of the arguments presented in the literature. Set up a class discussion or debate to exchange and clarify viewpoints.

You are probably beginning to realize how complex it can be to plan for music teaching, and how difficult it is to plan effectively. If there is too great an emphasis on musical content, students may be intimidated or poorly motivated, and if there is too much emphasis on students, musical growth may be minimal. Ultimately the need is for a comprehensive approach to planning that relates the properties of music to the experiences of students via an expanding range of educational behaviors. This brings us to the fourth level of planning, namely, planning musical experiences.

LEVEL FOUR PLANNING: EXPERIENCES

The purpose of this level of planning is to ensure that educational experiences are musical and musical experiences are educational. Level Four Planning draws together multidimensional goals derived from the foregoing principles, aims, and objectives and relates those goals to the kinds of interactive behaviors that are necessary for linking music and students. Figure 12 indicates in broad terms the relationships among these three components. It recognizes the principle that educative behaviors provide the linkage between the tonal properties of music and the human experiences of students, and therefore that all three must be taken into account in planning. It is not enough to know and love music, nor is it sufficient only to know and love students. We also must have the educational technique to link students and music in an enduring, growth relationship.

As planners, we teachers have to ask ourselves which musical properties and which human experiences are to be the focus of attention in the classroom; which are to be brought together via educative behaviors at any given time. In our planning as well as teaching efforts along these lines we are faced again with the matter of effective verbal communication. Each of the nine subdivisions of figure 12 provides us with a fairly distinct vocabulary to facilitate and clarify such communication. These vocabularies take on particular value and importance at the Level Four Experience stage of planning, so let us re-emphasize them at this point.

Physical properties include words such as pitch, timbre, breathing, embouchure, articulation, diction, posture, fingering, bowing, attack, release, duration, vibration, intensity, reverberation, staccato, legato,

Figure 12 The Components of Level Four Planning*

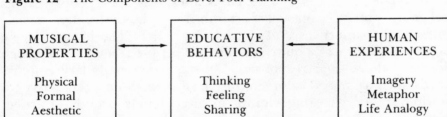

MUSICAL PROPERTIES	EDUCATIVE BEHAVIORS	HUMAN EXPERIENCES
Physical Formal Aesthetic	Thinking Feeling Sharing	Imagery Metaphor Life Analogy

*Variation 1 on Figure 3

marcato, intonation, and so forth. These are words that explain the nature of sound and the ways in which sound can be produced.

Formal properties include words such as melody. rhythm, harmony, tone, texture, tonality, crescendo, accent, dynamics, rubato, and their combinations such as phrase, binary, coda, fugue, sonata, symphony, and so forth.

Aesthetic properties include words such as shape, space, design, pattern, line, color, density, direction, unity, variety, subtlety, style, variation, balance, clarity, and perspective. An aesthetic vocabulary describes the results of the interactions that develop between and within the formal properties of music.

It is clear that the properties of the object, namely, music, are characterized by what can be termed a professional vocabulary. It is a vocabulary that musicians use to talk about the music they rehearse and perform; it is basically objective and precise. The properties themselves can be identified aurally or visually on a score, or, by what a performer does when the music is actually being produced. This is a specialized language that deals with the physical aspects of musical phenomena. It does not deal with the human response to those phenomena and so, in order to teach students as well as music, we need a second vocabulary that deals with the human response, a vocabulary we have termed experiential.

People experience music in many different ways. Sometimes they hear music and are aware of isolated properties but do not think about what they are hearing: sometimes they think about music and also have a feelingful response to it; sometimes they may not hear the music or be conscious of listening to it so much as feeling it; sometimes they may think about their feelingful response; they may also imagine as a result of thinking about or feeling the music, even though what they imagine may carry their minds away from the actual sound perception.

What kinds of words do we use to describe our responses to music? As we found in earlier chapters, an experiential vocabulary best describes these responses and may be subdivided into three major areas: image, metaphor, and life analog. When people choose a vocabulary drawn from imagery to describe their musical response, they may use words related to colors, shapes, landscapes, seascapes, people, events (religious, patriotic, martial, pastoral, domestic, or foreign), space, animals, the supernatural, sports, and so forth. The image may be vague and abstract or quite specific, but people frequently use such words to share their responses. A metaphoric vocabulary employs words such as angry, calm, confused, disturbed, energetic, excited, flowing, frantic, charging, vibrant, inspired, lonely, proud, refreshed, reverent, scared, and a host of other words that capture shades of feeling or movement generated by the musical events (generally as a result of physical congruity, association, and/or enculturation).

A third vocabulary within the experiential category is more abstract but nonetheless vitally important to music and to human development. This vocabulary describes our experiences with life and the living process. It includes words such as stability, growth, gravitation, deviation, complexity, expectation, relaxation, consistency, decay, distortion, extension, inhibition, modification, momentum, novelty, and cohesion. Again, these are words that do not describe musical phenomena but they do describe the human response to those phenomena. They are words that teach us about ourselves and the ways we relate to music, to art, and to other people.

> Think about the music teachers you have had and their use of professional, behavioral, and experiential vocabularies. To what extent do you think the usage was intentional and preplanned, or was it spontaneous and accidental?

Another major vocabulary describes educative behaviors. When we describe musical behaviors we tend to limit them to singing, playing instruments, reading music, composing, moving to music, or listening. In fact there are probably hundreds of behaviors that we touch on as we process music. These behaviors may be grouped in three broad subcategories of thinking, feeling, and sharing. When we analyze, define, locate, compare, relate, identify, classify, list, or compile, we are probably involved primarily in thinking about music; these are behaviors that tend to be systematic, convergent, and linear in nature. When we explore, imagine, sense, improvise, search, experiment, modify, or respond, we are probably involved primarily in feeling behaviors, behaviors that tend to be more spontaneous, divergent, intuitive, imaginative, and nonlinear in nature.

Then there are the sharing behaviors that include telling, performing, showing, conducting, moving, accompanying, asking, interacting, and expressing. These behaviors are characterized by social, dynamic, give-and-take relationships.

> To what extent have sharing behaviors played a significant role in your music education? And, were these behaviors truly reciprocal?

You will quickly realize these behaviors do not take place in isolation from one another but often in a rapid succession of emphases; however, for limited periods of time we can concentrate on one kind of behavior, so that the particular behavior receives special emphasis.

To recap for a moment, we have three basic components represented in the Level Four planning process; they are music, students, and interacting educative behaviors. This planning may be defined as the process of relating properties of the object (music) to experiences of the subject (student) via a range of appropriate behaviors (education).

Now for some examples. Let us assume we wish to deal with the musical property, crescendo. The crescendo is the basis of the musical event so to speak. What are the human experiences that might best relate to crescendo? Probably excitement, tension, and growth, words drawn from the experiential vocabulary. But what kinds of behaviors will draw the human and musical components together? Why not discuss, imagine, extend, discover, and demonstrate the various aspects and possibilities of crescendos? The "plan" can be represented as in figure 13. In these examples the musical events become educational when the bridges or linkage between the musical properties and the human experiences have been built via the educative behaviors. That is not to say behaviors should be limited to those that are identified or that human experience should not embrace additional interactions. On the contrary, the plan provides for educational opportunities; it does not limit them, but cannot guarantee them.

Obviously in order to plan in this way, teachers need to be articulate and have a vivid vocabulary of their own to draw on. Generally this has not been a high priority in music teacher preparation. Most class levels, particularly in elementary schools, have lists of recommended words for each age and maturational level, and wise planning takes this into account.

Level Four Experience planning stresses the central role of the

Figure 13   Examples of Interdependent Vocabularies for Level Four Planning

	Musical Properties ⟷	Educative Behaviors ⟷	Human Experiences
Example 1	Crescendo ⟷	Discuss Imagine Extend ⟷ Discover Demonstrate	Tension Growth Expansion Excitement
Example 2	Fingering ⟷	Explore Identify Recognize ⟷ Practice Demonstrate	Flow Clarity Relaxation Consistency
Example 3	Timbre ⟷	Explore Experiment Substitute ⟷ Intensify	Blend Contrast Soothing Vibrant

educative behaviors because the nature of the behaviors determines the nature of the program as well as the characteristic qualities of those students who graduate from it. Regardless of the particular emphasis that may emerge in a program, such as skills or knowledge or values, the three components—musical properties, human experiences, and educational behaviors—should be articulated in all programs. For example, let us supply a few words in each of the three vocabularies, as in figure 14.

> Select a song that your classmates might enjoy. Choose words from the three basic vocabularies that you believe to be appropriate for teaching the song. Rehearse the song using the selected vocabularies and evaluate the results.

Now that we have examined four levels of planning for music teaching, you probably will have realized that no single stratum is sufficient unto itself. To plan effectively we need a philosophy and

Figure 14 Relationships Among Musical Properties, Educational Behaviors, and Human Experiences

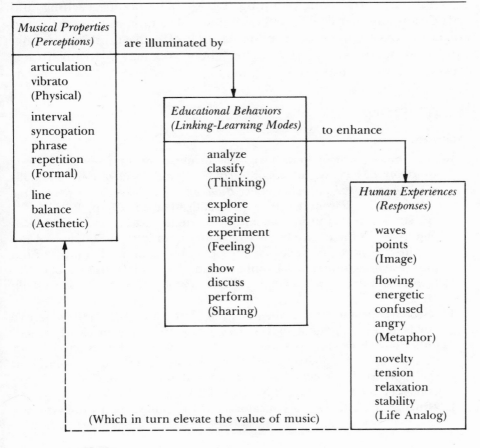

principles that provide a sense of direction for a program; we need a program with aims that support and define the limits of our operation; we need specific objectives within a program to provide clear short-term goals; and finally we need a planning structure that will allow experiences to become truly musical and truly educative.

In this latter respect it should be noted that if experiential lesson plans are too detailed, they are likely to be inflexible and the teacher may forget parts of them anyway! If they are too sparse, they may not provide the guidance to keep the lesson on course. Different teachers will have different needs and thus employ different, individual formats in this respect. It is the responsibility of the teacher to translate his or her plans into action. Every teacher will do that in unique ways based on immediate as well longer-range diagnoses of students' musical needs, and on the selection of personal teaching behaviors to meet those needs. A more general caveat would be that, like a well-structured symphonic movement, a good lesson plan usually includes introduction, development, and recapitulation sections, replete with points of repetition and contrast, climax and resolution, excitement and fulfillment.

A final word about planning, but actually about teaching and education in general: Plan on a lifetime of learning as you teach, and plan on working to become an increasingly effective thinking, feeling, and sharing person as you teach. Then, you may plan on a most rewarding life in music education.

EXTENSIONS

Statements

1. "In general, instructional programs in music suffer from three basic shortcomings: (1) vagueness of purpose, (2) misplaced emphasis and (3) lack of sequence." Sidnell, Robert, *Building Instructional Programs in Music Education* (Englewood Cliffs, N.J.: Prentice-Hall, 1973), p. 12.
2. "In student-centered instruction the students assist in the selection of objectives, in the choice of subject matter, and in the evaluation of the results. In short, they exercise the optimum amount of control of the total learning situation." Leonhard, Charles, and House, Robert W., *Foundations and Principles of Music Education* (New York: McGraw-Hill, 1972), p. 277.
3. "Broadly speaking, the younger the child the shorter term the objective needs to be; but long or short term, the objective must be clearly stated. Otherwise, how can he know what to aim for? If the objective is not clearly stated, the question might be not 'how am I doing?' but 'am I on the right road?' or even 'on the map?' " Bentley, Arnold, *Music in Education* (Windsor, England: NFER Publishing Co., 1975), p. 69.
4. "During the late 1960's educators and the public increasingly sensed

discrepancies between high sounding educational goals and student performance. Upon closer examination, the objectives appeared so vague and elusive that educators and critics of schools lacked common ground for assessing the effectiveness of education and for planning what many considered an urgently needed revitalization." Von Haden, Herbert I., and King, Jean Marie, *Innovations in Education* (Worthington, Ohio: Charles A. Jones, 1971), p. 46.

5. "Even though the development and evaluation of objectives in the affective domain are somewhat more difficult to design, they should be included in planning for music instruction." Nye, Robert Evans, and Nye, Vernice Trousdale, *Essentials of Teaching Elementary School Music* (Englewood Cliffs, N.J.: Prentice-Hall, 1974), p. 38.

Questions and Suggestions

1. Interview a music teacher and ask him or her the following questions: What kinds of planning techniques do you employ? Does your planning focus on the diagnosis of student needs or musical needs or both? Compare your results with those of other students in your class.

2. Question some teachers about their philosophies of music education. Can you discover the principles underlying those philosophies, principles that might relate to man, music, or education?

3. Write several principles drawn from your philosophy of music education. Think about the varied functions music serves in society and to what extent music education should relate to those functions. This will help focus your thinking.

4. Examine some basic texts or curriculum guides and list the aims of their programs. Evaluate their strengths and weaknesses.

5. Interview two or three teachers who are responsible for similar music programs, perhaps a secondary choral program or a junior high string program. In what ways do the aims of their programs differ? Have these differences simply emerged or are they clearly the result of different principles and philosophies?

6. You might wish to evaluate your own level of conceptual understanding at this point. One means for doing this would be to list all the subconcepts of melody or tonality or rhythm you can think of and then arrange them in a developmental order. To what extent can you agree on the developmental order in your class?

7. Locate some classroom texts designed for use at different levels of the school system. Examine some of the objectives suggested for individual lessons and attempt to derive the principles underlying those objectives. Also determine to what extent there is a recognizable flow from general principles planning through to more specific aims and objectives.

8. Take one objective and list as many experiences as you can devise to realize the objective. Couch your experiences in terms of questions as well as statements.

9. Build a repertoire of sounds and discuss the characteristics of each. Create the sounds in different orders and discuss their possible use in association with different colors, movements, and pictures. Build a pic-

ture in sound and try to capture the quality of feeling of the picture in the quality of feeling in the composition.

10. What are some of the ways you would plan to involve a child's creative initiative in your elementary program?

11. Using a choral selection, devise a series of experiences that focus on imagining, producing, perceiving, and responding to the music.

12. Find examples of pictures, poems, stories, movements, or experiences you would use to motivate composing in an elementary classroom. Develop a list of images, ideas, or feelings that could be used as a source of motivation or inspiration for some compositions.

13. Plan a brief lesson sequence for a listening experience emphasizing a professional vocabulary. Using the same literature, plan a second sequence emphasizing an experiential vocabulary. Teach the lessons to two classes of similar age and background. Evaluate the results.

14. Planning for music education involves words. Make a list of words that you use most frequently when you are rehearsing or practicing or just responding to a musical experience. Can you classify the words in groups according to their function? Invent some categories of your own if you wish and then consider which words would be most appropriate for use in planning.

15. Examine some curriculum guides and text series paying particular attention to the behavioral vocabularies reflected in the statements of objectives. Based on your own behaviors and experiences with music, to what extent do the desired behaviors represent comprehensive and vital musical experiences? What learning modes do those behaviors most frequently represent?

16. How complete is your conceptual grasp of music at this time? Make a list of professional terms (professional vocabulary) that you feel you could demonstrate, terms such as rubato, dissonance, interval, and so forth. Compare your list with those of other students. Develop a group listing and then consider which words you would expect children of different ages to be familiar with.

17. View a videotape of a music lesson. Make a list of the behavioral vocabulary that is employed. Is it sparse or extensive? How would the lesson have been affected if the desired behaviors had been more or less obvious? Plan a lesson segment in which you pay great attention to the behavioral vocabulary. Now teach the lesson to two groups of students of similar age and background. In the first instance minimize the use of the behavioral vocabulary and in the second instance, emphasize it. Evaluate the results.

18. Planning is in essence distinguishing between what might and what should happen. Do you feel your music education thus far has been characterized more by careful planning than by chance? Does our profession as a whole operate more by chance than by rigorous planning? Why?

19. We know that music with immediate appeal may have limited staying power, but, on the other hand, it often takes time to recognize and enjoy

more complex and substantive music. Can we account for such different situations with careful planning? What would you do?

20. Some aspects of music programs are constant in the sense that they need to be ongoing in order to ensure growth and insight. Other aspects can be short-term and involve relatively independent projects. Give some examples of both aspects of a program and of how you might incorporate them into a program of your choice.

21. What do you know of music education in other countries and other cultures? Undertake some library research and try to determine the extent to which principles of music education differ from one society to another and even within a society from one community to another. Provide some examples of how different principles lead to different experiences in a music program.

22. You are now familiar with the four levels of planning we have considered: principles, aims, objectives, and experiences. Following are the words and music to a lullaby entitled "Wao" that originated in the African country of Zaire. Some basic background information on "Wao" and several sample discussion questions are provided at the end of this section. Develop a lesson plan for an elementary level general music class using this song and related material as a basis for your lesson:

A. Consider and specify briefly how the materials fit in with particular principles, aims, and objectives of your (hypothetical) program.

B. Consider and specify the sequence of experiences for the lesson. This will be the order of student activities and behaviors that are deemed most appropriate for the objective(s) being addressed.

C. When structuring the experiences, be particularly careful about choosing key words from the three vocabularies, and note these in your plan.

D. Give thought to the use of nonverbal behaviors. Where in the lesson might physical or musical modeling be called for? Perhaps syllabizing might be introduced to stress or clarify a conceptual or expressive meaning. In any event, note nonverbal behavior possibilities at appropriate points in your plan.

E. Specify your evaluation ideas for determining the effectiveness of the lesson.

When you have done this, undertake a similar assignment by selecting some band, choral, or orchestral literature for a secondary school program and build one or several lesson plans around that literature. Then, compare your finished plans with more traditional models in curriculum guides, music text series, or other music texts. Finally, share and discuss the fruits of this exercise with your class colleagues.

Background Material for "Wao": "Wao" (wah-oh) is an imitation of the way a baby cries. In this case, it is also the title of a lullaby, and lullabies have a purpose. Their steady rhythm and repetition are lulling assur-

WAO*

Kikongo

Wa- o, wa- o, wa,
ba- by, you go to sleep,
lit- tle black ba- by, oh,
lit- tle black ba- by, oh,
E- lam- bi- di.

Wa- o, wa- o, wa,
ba- by, you go to sleep,
lit- tle black ba- by, oh,
lit- tle black ba- by, oh,
E- lam- bi- di.

Now don't you weep.
Soon we will eat.
I'm al- ways near.

Close your black eyes and
Dad- dy's a' com- ing,
On ma- ma's back you

don't make a peep.
he caught some meat.
don't need to fear.

On the last verse, repeat the last measure several times, softer and softer, to a whisper (Elambidi).

Just go to sleep.
(E- lam- bi- di.)

*Transcribed and translated by Ruby Wiebe.

Sample Congo Drum or Tom-Tom Accompaniment Figures—Improvise Others:

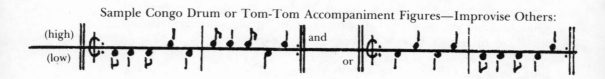

(high)
(low)

and

or

ances of mother's nearness and protection, as well as a masking of other noises. No baby in a remote village of Zaire has a crib. The infant takes naps tied to mother's back as she works outdoors amidst the bustle and noise of the village. This song also reminds us that there is no supermarket nearby. Father goes out into the forest to hunt for meat or gather honey, while mother gardens or does other family chores.

Much use of repetition and syncopated rhythm is a common characteristic of Central African songs. Notice the frequent repetition of the syncopated rhythm pattern first heard in measure four. This lends great unity to the music. Of course, too much repetition tends to make people drowsy, but, in this case, that is the idea. So, much repetition is a good thing in a lullaby. Can you think of an American or Western lullaby that contains much repetition of musical elements? Probably this is easy; however, can you think of one that has a fast tempo and employs much syncopation like this example does? Could part of the reason for the difference in musical sound be that in America a lullaby usually is heard in a quiet bedroom while in rural Zaire it is generally sung in a rather noisy, motion-filled environment for a child wrapped to its mother's back?

REFERENCES AND READINGS

Bloom, Benjamin S.; Krathwohl, David R.; and Masia, Bertram B. *Taxonomy of Educational Objectives, The Classification of Educational Goals, Handbook I: Cognitive Domain.* New York: David McKay Co., 1956.

Boyle, David J. *Instructional Objectives in Music.* Vienna, Va.: Music Educators National Conference, 1974.

Bruner, Jerome S. *Toward a Theory of Instruction.* Cambridge: Harvard University Press, 1966.

Combs, Arthur W. *Educational Accountability: Beyond Behavioral Objectives.* Washington: Association for Supervision and Curriculum Development, 1973.

House, Robert W. "Curriculum Construction in Music Education." In *Basic Concepts in Music Education.* Chicago: National Society for the Study of Education, 57th Yearbook, 1958.

Krathwohl, David R.; Bloom, Benjamin S.; and Masia, Bertram B. *Taxonomy of Educational Objectives, The Classification of Educational Goals, Handbook II: Affective Domain.* New York: David McKay Co., 1964.

Krug, Edward A. *Curriculum Planning.* New York: Harper and Brothers, 1957.

Leonhard, Charles, and House, Robert W. *Foundations and Principles of Music Education.* New York: McGraw-Hill, 1972.

Music Educators National Conference (MENC). *Music in General Education,* edited by Karl D. Ernst and Charles L. Gary. Washington: MENC, 1965.

Music Educators National Conference (MENC). *Music in World Cultures.* Washington: MENC, 1972.

Music Educators National Conference (MENC). *The School Music Program: Description and Standards.* Vienna, Va.: MENC, 1974.

Paynter, John. *Hear and Now: An Introduction to Modern Music in School.* London: Universal, 1972.

Rogers, Carl C. *Freedom to Learn.* Columbus, Ohio: Charles E. Merrill, 1969.

Schwadron, Abraham A. *Aesthetics: Dimensions for Music Education.* Washington: Music
    Educators National Conference, 1966.
Sidnell, Robert. *Building Instructional Programs in Music Education.* Englewood Cliffs,
    N.J.: Prentice-Hall, 1973.
Tait, Malcolm J. *Comprehensive Musicianship Through Choral Performance, Vols. I & II.*
    Menlo Park, Calif: Addison-Wesley, 1973 & 1975.
Vulliamy, George. *Pop, Rock and Ethnic Music in School.* Cambridge: Cambridge Uni-
    versity Press, 1982.

7

Evaluation

Underlying Concepts: Evaluation is a method for determining the worth or value of an object or process. Evaluation feedback is essential to progress and improvement in the teaching-learning process.

While the more objective and quantitative aspects of evaluation have received considerable attention in music education research and practice, the more subjective, personal, and qualitative aspects need considerable development if a balanced and holistic approach is to be achieved.

Student evaluation is concerned with determining the nature and quality of students' musical experiences. It emphasizes the question of linkage between tonal-rhythmic phenomena and human experience and is concerned with growth developments in thinking, feeling, and sharing music.

Teacher evaluation is concerned with a teacher's ability to diagnose musical concerns and to select teaching strategies appropriate to those concerns in the context of the stated goals for the students of a particular program.

Program evaluation is concerned with the appropriateness of selected goals and methods, and the degree of progress apparent in achieving those goals. It examines the degree of support for a given program and the extent to which teacher and student behaviors are congruent with stated goals.

Evaluation is an essential accompaniment to planning-teaching-learning activities because without evaluation there can be no assurance of a progressive, orderly process of education. Evaluation provides for a feedback loop to planning, and the loop cannot be complete nor the educational process effective without it. Because music functions

among other ways as an art form, we might attempt to excuse ourselves from evaluation with the rationale that "artistic intangibles"
cannot be evaluated. But even if that were true for music, it would
not be true of music education and its effects.

As music educators, we are directly responsible and accountable
for the growth and development of human beings. Such accountability requires more than student evaluation; it requires teacher and
program evaluation as well. It requires more than test scores and
grade reports; it requires constant formal and informal observations,
needs assessments, self and program analyses, behavior scales, performance critiques, attitude assessments, achievement measures, and
a host of other creative and imaginative tools and techniques. It requires more than the summative evaluations needed to assess general
levels of goal attainment; it also requires formative evaluations to
facilitate the fairly specific diagnoses that guide further instructional
planning.

The learner, the teacher, and the program are the basic components of formal education. Though they are by no means discrete
variables, we must evaluate them frequently and imaginatively in our
efforts to develop effective practices and humane, musical beings—
thinking, feeling, and sharing persons. As mentioned earlier, life
without wise choosing and using, without qualitative valuing and evaluating would at best be aimless, and very likely disastrous. So would
the life-enhancing process of music education.

EVALUATION EMPHASES

Evaluation in music education has focused primarily on the perception of tonal-rhythmic phenomena, the ability to identify tonal-rhythmic
properties, or the ability to produce such musical phenomena. In
general, the process has been carefully structured, objectified, and,
perhaps most tellingly, it has been quantified. It is a process that has
paralleled evaluative techniques in other areas of human endeavor
for the kinds of reasons discussed in earlier chapters; namely, we as
human beings have been particularly interested and concerned with
exploring and cataloging our external world, including our perception of tonal-rhythmic phenomena, because the process corresponds
with the kinds of logical, deductive thought processes that education
in our Western civilization has striven to develop in us.

Evaluation of the psychological or affective processes in music has
not received the same degree of attention even though these processes
represent an integral part of the musical experience. As we have seen,
the inner responses to music are often flowing or even fleeting impres-
sions that can be difficult to verbalize and document. Nevertheless,

the holistic nature and quality of the musical experience certainly should be the primary concern of music education. Therefore, the challenge facing us in evaluation is to examine not only the perception of musical phenomena, and the psychological responses to those phenomena, but also the kinds and qualities of experience that develop as a result of such perceptive-affective interactions and linkages.

> Listen to a piece of music. Try to determine how the nature and quality of the experience varies when you concentrate in three different ways: on the musical properties of the object; on the responses of the subject—your responses; and on the flow and interplay between the object's musical properties and your subjective, personal reactions.

Tests that have dealt with the phenomenological process include tests of musical "aptitude" and "ability" such as the Seashore *Measures of Musical Talents,* the Wing *Standardized Tests of Musical Intelligence,* the Bentley *Measures of Musical Ability,* and the Gordon *Musical Aptitude Profile,* to name just a few of the better known tests. There also are nationally standardized music "achievement" tests such as the Aliferis *Music Achievement Test,* the Colwell *Elementary Music Achievement Tests,* the Snyder Knuth *Music Achievement Test* and the more recent music test portions of the National Assessment of Educational Progress.

When we come to the psychological dimension of the musical experience, we find relatively few tests. In 1934 Kate Hevner (Mueller) did pioneer work in the area. Paul Farnsworth, George Kyme, and Newell Long have added some notable efforts. Test items have included check lists of "mood" words and performances of brief musical phrases in which subjects are asked to select superior versions. The latter type of item also is included in the Gordon *Musical Aptitude Profile.* However, such items tend to limit the responses of the subjects by forcing them to make selections based on an assumption that one performance or response is better than another, an assumption that sometimes is difficult to substantiate. Nevertheless, within their stated purposes such tests have been and can be very informative.

In essence, however, if we are truly concerned with evaluating the nature and value of students' musical experiences, attention must focus not only on the effectiveness of perception, and on the nature of the response, but also on the interactive relationships between the two.* In other words we are arguing that the quality of a musical experience is dependent upon the nature of the linkage that develops

*For two recent efforts in this direction, see Haack, P. A., "A Study of High School Music Participants' Stylistic Preferences and Identification Abilities in Music and the Visual Arts," *Journal of Research in Music Education* (Winter 1982, vol. 30, no. 4, pp. 213–220); and "The Influence of Instruction on Student Self-Awareness and Valuing of Varying Music and Art Styles" (paper by the same author, presented at MENC, Miami, 1980).

between the perception of the musical phenomena and the human response to those phenomena. For example, we know of people who can process musical events, as consumers or as producers, with a high degree of accuracy and fluency; but their degree of personal investment in those events is minimal, and consequently the musical experiences tend to be somewhat limited or shallow by their own admission. Similarly, there are people whose personal involvement in musical events is extraordinarily high but their processing of those events, quite low. For example, listeners who become affectively immersed and dream their way through a performance, or performers who discharge enormous amounts of physical or emotional energy at the expense of stylistic integrity fall into this group. Their resultant musical experiences are somewhat unbalanced and limited.

In considering the evaluation of music students, teachers, and programs, it is important that we keep in mind the unique, complex, and holistic nature of musical experience. In doing so, we are more likely to do justice to the relationships and interdependence of musical processes and human processes within our educational processes. Many of the references and readings listed at the conclusion of this chapter provide useful information about the specifics and details of developing evaluative methods and instruments for teachers' individual needs. What follows in this chapter is a more general framework of ideas to guide the development of such methods and materials toward a more balanced and holistic approach than that which is normally taken. It still remains for individual teachers to develop truly creative applications of this information, applications that are program specific, and that take into balanced account *all* of the principles and goals of the specific program.

Arrange to take a test of musical achievement, and discuss the strengths and weaknesses of the process: How would you modify and/or expand the test if you wished it to represent more accurately the way you experience music? How would you change it to represent more accurately the holistic goals of music education emphasized here?

STUDENT EVALUATION

We know from research as well as from our own teaching experience that people vary quite dramatically in the range of their musical experiences. For example, some people feel musical experiences quite powerfully, but it may not occur to them that thinking and sharing behaviors are available or appropriate, and that these behaviors may profoundly influence the quality and value of their musical experiences. In contrast, some people approach musical experiences in highly analytical ways, and may be afraid even to admit the possibility of a feelingful involvement with music. For some people the musical experience is essentially personal and private; for others it may be quite open, with a general willingness to participate in group activities or share responses to a particular musical event.

Range of Behaviors

Clearly when people hear music they have a wide choice of behaviors available to them. They may elect, consciously or subconsciously, to hear (which includes "listen" and "identify") how the music is produced. The focus of this attention may be on the physical aspects of sound production, on articulation, breathing, bowing, finger action, or on some other technical aspect. They may hear all kinds of subtleties connected with the actual sound production that would escape the hearing of other people.

Another choice of behavior might involve hearing the formal elements of music including rhythm, melody, and harmony, tone, and so forth. This also includes hearing relating to subcategories of elements such as syncopation, rubato, portamento, accent, dissonance, and a host of other aspects within the larger elemental categories. People may also hear other formal properties of musical events, those that serve a cohesive function such as repetition, variation, transition, development; or perhaps they may hear first and second subjects, themes, recapitulations, countersubjects, and codas. Thus they might be led to attend to how the musical elements interact with one another to produce patterns, shapes, styles, and genres that are aesthetically pleasing and unique.

People who are able to perceive all of the above in a given period of time exhibit a wide range of musical behaviors. However, we know from earlier discussions that when people experience music, they generally do more than just objectively perceive it. They in fact bring something of themselves to what they are hearing, and it is that subjective something that also must concern us here.

As in perceiving music, so too in responding there are conscious or subconscious choices of alternative behaviors. An early or first choice often involves the substitution of some kind of image for the sounds, or substitution of some occurrence, place, person, product, color, or shape. If this alternative is selected, then attention often shifts to the image; the image is experienced rather than the music, and to the extent that this occurs, other musical information is likely to be bypassed.

A second choice involves experiencing a feeling metaphor with the music, a parallel association in the sense that the music is heard but it is also felt. As an example, thick harmonic densities heard fortissimo may be felt and experienced as anger. In this sense the metaphor is not a substitute for the musical events, it parallels them. In the same way, such choice may involve experiencing the music as a movement metaphor, a quality such as lively, majestic, controlled, quick, or smooth. Here the parallel association is between what is heard and a quality of movement that is experienced. These metaphoric behaviors are for the most part fleeting and transitory; they do not represent an abandonment of the musical event so much as an internalizing of it, a process of making the events more personal.

A third choice may involve experiencing a life analogy with the music. This is not a substitution of one behavior for another, or even a paralleling of one behavior with another. Here we experience an identity with the music. The life analog is characterized by qualities of expectancy, deviation, inhibition, tension, growth, gravitation, direction, relief, confirmation, and a host of other qualities that are common to life processes and musical processes. Figure 15 graphically summarizes the potential range of musical behaviors discussed above.

Discuss (a) the varying extent to which people actually exercise musical choices; (b) the ways in which such choices may be limited by narrow concepts about music fostered by enculturation including education; and (c) the ways in which choices can be expanded via education. Can you share examples of how your own choices for interactions with and uses of music have been limited, or expanded?

These examples of musical perceptions and responses represent a range of potential behaviors within a musical experience. However, in and of themselves they do not determine the quality of a musical experience. In other words, a checklist of image, metaphor, and life-analog words will not necessarily help to determine the qualitative worth of a musical experience. However, it.can represent a first level of assessment activity in student evaluation since a student who is able to incorporate a wide range of such behaviors in a musical experience

Figure 15   Potential Musical Behaviors

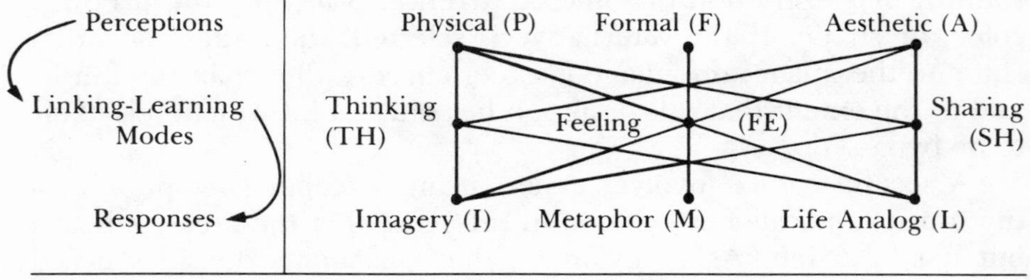

has demonstrated a prime requisite and thus potential for qualitative growth. (See figure 9 in chapter 5 for an example of such an evaluative checklist.)

Intensity of Behaviors

In order to raise evaluation beyond this point, we need to direct our attention toward what might be called the intensity of the musical experience. There is a kind of intensity, or degree of involvement, within all musical experience that plays a significant role in determining the meaning and value of that experience. Intensity may vary from indifference on the one hand to total absorption on the other. An example comes to mind concerning two people who differ on the relative "goodness" of a particular musical experience. If each person had approximately similar ranges of perception and response, but only one thought the performance was particularly rewarding, that one probably did so on the basis of the personal intensity of the musical experience. In other words, that person was more fully absorbed in all behaviors without loss of interest or concentration; he was involved from start to finish. The other person was probably involved with the music from time to time; interest was aroused for short periods, but periods of distraction or boredom also crept in. For this person the musical experience could hardly be characterized as intense. Is this a possible and logical analysis of these contrasting experiences?

Perhaps the most reasonable explanation for such intensity contrasts (although it is yet to be supported by detailed research) is that only minimal intensity develops when musical behaviors are disparate and isolated. Under such conditions, it is easy for distractions to intrude. On the other hand, when perceptions and responses are developed and related into a more complex network of interacting behaviors, via thinking, feeling, and sharing, then the situation is ripe for growth in intensity. This after all is a condition that is observable in other forms of human behavior: Within the capabilities of the subject, as more sensory inputs become stimulated and as the network of neural activity grows in complexity, there tends to be a self-feeding crescendo of vigor, of interest, of eagerness and concentration.

> Consider how the Aristotelian Principle (an older hypothesis, but also in need of detailed research) might relate to this explanation. The Aristotelian Principle says that persons enjoy using their innate and trained abilities, and the resulting satisfaction grows as their abilities are developed, or as the material to which they are applied grows in complexity . . . within their competence limits.

Quality of Behaviors

The key to increased meaning then is not increased experience per se, but rather increased significance of experience; disparate information needs to be related in order for it to become meaningful and valuable. Similarly, as musical perception feeds into musical response, and is in turn nourished by response, so linkage develops. Accordingly, so does intensity, meaning, and value. Thus we are equating qualitative musical experiences with the range and intensity of the musical behaviors within those experiences, and with the ways in which those multiple musical behaviors relate to and impinge upon one another.

Recall one of your most *intense* musical experiences. How can you best describe it? What words, which vocabularies would you employ? Was the intensity of the musical experience related to the music, the setting, the performers, the state of your mind, all or none of these?

In figure 16, X equals a musical event. The rather isolated behaviors on the left tend simply to grow from and encircle that event in a relatively independent manner. At this point the behaviors are quite disparate and not necessarily related, and therefore intensity is minimal. For the quality of the musical experience to grow or heighten, the behaviors need linkage; that is, they need to begin to interact and become related with one another via the linking-learning modes of thinking, feeling, and sharing. Thus intensity should increase, and our diagram may be modified as on the right.

Within a musical event, if the range of perception is simply Physical or Formal, *or* the range of response is limited to Imagery or Metaphor and these responses and perceptions are unrelated, then the intensity of the experience will tend to be quite a bit less than possible, and the meaning and quality of the experience will probably be shallow. If, on the other hand, within the same musical event the range of perception were to include Physical, Formal, and Aesthetic, *and* the range of response were to include Imagery, Metaphor, and Life Analogies, *and* these behaviors were to be effectively focused and filtered through THinking, FEeling, and SHaring learning modes with linkage developing between the behaviors, then it is safe to assume the experience would achieve a high degree of intensity. The quality of the experience could then be characterized as having breadth, depth, substance, and excellence.

The functional component or corollary of experiential quality also can be evaluated in terms of range and depth. The range of needs and uses for which music can be employed certainly is of importance

Figure 16   Quality Levels of Musical Behaviors

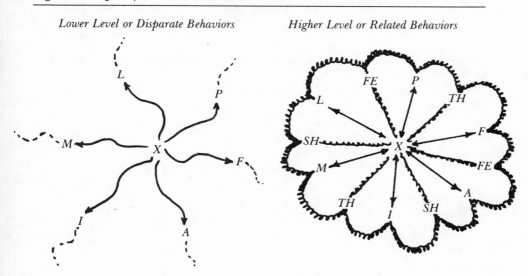

Lower Level or Disparate Behaviors   *Higher Level or Related Behaviors*

in evaluating the musical competence of persons. However, the intensity or depth of the applications, that is, the appropriateness and effective linkage of the chosen music to the use or need circumstances in which it is employed, must be considered as well. In this sense, heightened "values awareness" is an important teaching-learning concern, as it must be in the more general sense as well. This fact is becoming increasingly clear as we understand more about how our values determine our behaviors. The growth cycle here has to do with the fact that values dictate uses and effective uses enhance values.

While we have mentioned the importance of musical values and valuing throughout the text, we should emphasize that the purpose is not to tell students what to value, for that is tantamount to behavior control. The purpose is to help them realize the range of potential values and understand the principles of effective musical use for the depth vital to quality life experiences for themselves and others. Figure 17 provides an example of a values awareness exercise that can also serve feedback-evaluation purposes. Similar teaching and evaluating ideas can be gleaned from many available texts on values and values clarification.

Summary

Frequent evaluation via various forms of student assessment and feedback is essential to improvement of the teaching-learning process in music education. Our primary evaluative goal should be to determine the quality of our students' musical experiences and their related growth developments in thinking, feeling, and sharing music. This

Figure 17   Evaluating Musical Values

How useful is music to me for:	Not Used				Very Useful		Style and Example
	0	1	2	3	4	5	
1. Understanding or clarifying (my own feelings)							
2. Communicating feelings (e.g., love or concern)							
3. Light listening (with friends)							
4. Heavy listening (by myself)							
5. Background for special events (parents' silver anniversary)							
6. Background for social events (teen party in home)							
7. Masking effects and background (Covering noise distractions)							
8. Calming effects (when I'm uptight)							
9. Energizing effects (picker-upper when down)							
10. Reducing boredom (when driving, doing routine work)							

can be achieved by first determining the range of behaviors within given experiences and by next determining the degree of intensity, the extent of the linkage between those behaviors. Generally the evaluative models used in music education have been rather narrowly conceived. There is a real need to develop more comprehensive models and materials to do greater justice to student evaluation.

Given a holistic conceptual framework and some creative thought, practicing professionals can develop materials and carry on such evaluation activities in an effective manner appropriate to their own curricula and classrooms. Particularly encouraging and helpful in this respect is the emerging field of "naturalistic" inquiry, observation, and evaluation which should be considered in the research, measurement, and test components of all contemporary teacher education curricula. Naturalistic approaches, with their strong and credible provisions for the humanistic-qualitative aspects of inquiry, valuing, and evaluation, will be of great help in rounding out our current assessment methods and materials (See the readings listed under Guba at the conclusion of this chapter.)

Make some suggestions as to how music education might more adequately evaluate the quality of musical experiences. Could your suggestions be incorporated into an assessment procedure? Attempt to devise methods including teacher observation checklists, student self-analysis forms, structured interviews and so forth, and experiment with their use on your class colleagues.

TEACHER EVALUATION

Criteria for effective teaching are highly complex and are frequently influenced by, if not confused by, reference to who we are rather than to what we do. While personality or individual characteristics can contribute to teaching effectiveness, it is perhaps wiser to direct our evaluative search toward job function, which is after all the most distinctive and distinguishable mark of professionalism. So in considering teacher evaluation we need to focus on the teaching act rather than on the teacher per se.

Diagnosis

If we only see them once a week, and then in a large class, it can be tremendously difficult for us to know our students as individuals. Yet such knowledge is a fundamental requirement for sound and effective teaching in any area. Any means we can devise to gain a more comprehensive insight into the lives and characters of our students will help teaching effectiveness. This argument cannot be overstated. When we begin to see students as individuals, we begin to see how each can contribute to and benefit from the total learning mosaic. This is especially so in music education. Each child has a unique investment to make in a group, a unique insight and quality to share that not only helps the group but also strengthens his or her own sense of self-identity. Music can facilitate the growth process, provided that the musical activities and the musical content are congruent with student interests and needs. So the second fundamental requirement is to know the music.

There is a constant challenge to balance individual needs with the comprehensive nature of the subject so that students can move forward technically, expressively, and conceptually. This is why we need to develop an awareness of the musical concerns within our classes and lessons as they unfold from week to week. Part of the evaluative process should involve a record of the relative amounts of time spent in developing technical skills, conceptual understanding, and expressive sensitivity. You may find, for example, that excessive concentration on one of these areas can lead to stagnation in others. More noticeably perhaps, students may lose interest quickly unless they are encouraged to relate what they do to what they hear and to what they feel. This can be achieved by maintaining a balance among the three basic concerns in the music lesson. For example, a lesson that is devoted entirely to technical concerns will obviously place great demands on children whose technical accomplishments are only minimally developed. Similarly, a heavy emphasis on conceptual development through analytical listening may lead to a loss of focus and concentration as well as to restlessness particularly among younger students. As teachers, we all have areas of strength and our own special interests. If we believe musical expression is of major importance, our students may in fact be led to develop great expressiveness, but hopefully not as mere imitators, at the expense of the knowledge of what they are doing, nor how or why they are doing it.

It is important in evaluating our own teaching that we keep a clear and even perspective on the musical concerns we choose to diagnose. When we do this, we are likely to encourage balanced growth in our students' abilities to think, feel, share, and generally interact with music more effectively. Our students' balanced musical growth is a most basic criterion for our own evaluation as well as that of our students and our programs in general.

Listen to two or three instrumental and/or choral rehearsals and make a list of the concerns diagnosed by the teacher-director. Reflect on the reasons for those diagnoses and the extent to which members of the ensembles were made aware of those particular concerns.

Verbal Behaviors

Music educators have not developed the kind of precision vocabularies that are characteristic of some professions. Indeed, it may be argued that as a profession, we have not recognized the importance nor the potential power of language as a tool for assisting musical understanding. More frequently than not, our verbal phrases have tended to be spontaneous and perhaps vague rather than carefully selected and relevant to the musical tasks at hand. Some music educators are becoming aware of this shortcoming, however. Jerrold Ross (1978) states that music teachers must "come to grips with their feelings and, by exploring them deeply be able to communicate them in words to others. After all, how else can a teacher teach? . . . The assertion that the arts are essentially nonverbal merely provides the teacher with a convenient excuse for not knowing" (p. 82).

In an earlier chapter it was suggested we should employ three vocabularies in music education. The first is a professional vocabulary having to do with musical sound properties. The second is an experiential vocabulary having to do with internal responses to the sound properties. The third is a behavioral vocabulary having to do with those interactive behaviors between self and sound, the behaviors that might generally be subsumed under the categories of thinking, feeling, and sharing.

Just as we recognized potential problems with diagnoses, so there are dangers with verbal behaviors, especially in utilizing words that come easily rather than finding words that are most appropriate. It may be a revealing experience for us to listen to and evaluate a recording of our own teaching; this kind of evaluation should be done regularly. We may discover our vocabulary is very heavily weighted toward the professional category with minimal usage in the experiential area. We may also find our students are being encouraged to analyze or identify more frequently than they are being led to imagine or feel. Only by listening to ourselves very carefully are we going to know if our verbal behaviors are comprehensive, variable, and appropriate. If we are limited to no more than a half dozen experiential words, such as lively, slow, sad, moving, smooth, and happy, then we have some work to do.

If we are going to avoid verbal poverty, we need constantly to expand our professional vocabulary beyond the simple concepts of fast and slow or loud and soft. Students can provide valuable input into vocabulary development if they are given an opportunity to do so. This is where evaluation should address the relative weighting of questions and statements within a music lesson. Some teachers ask very few questions while others ask strings of questions but seem reluctant to ever make a statement. Some students ask questions while others feel too threatened or intimidated to question anything! The need is for dialog development that employs objective and subjective language, that involves questions as well as statements, and that seeks input from students as well as from teachers.

Nonverbal Behaviors

It is very difficult to evaluate nonverbal components of music teaching unless we have access to a videotape machine or to the kind of colleague who can watch us carefully and tell us about the nonverbal strategies we employ, both intentionally and unintentionally. One or both of these approaches to evaluation should be used regularly for as long as we remain professional educators. Many of us are simply unaware of the role our bodies play in assisting or hindering the teaching process. This is to be expected since only minimal attention has been given to nonverbal strategies in music teacher training and evaluation. Nevertheless, some teachers do provide physical modeling, aural modeling and musical modeling as naturally and as frequently as they employ words, while other teachers model only rarely. We should also be aware of the dangers of overmodeling in the sense of overwhelming the students. They may be so intimidated by a teacher's competence in music modeling, for example, that they feel little room for developing their own musical identities.

Perhaps the first thing to determine in this area is the extent and range of our nonverbal behaviors. For example, how frequently do we use our bodies to demonstrate an appropriate posture? How often do we utilize syllable sounds to provide an aural image of a particular articulation or tone quality? How often do we perform passages or even a complete composition for our students? Perhaps our natural inclination lies more toward aural modeling with syllables than with direct musical modeling, but, be that as it may, we need to raise our levels of consciousness in this area so that our choices are enlightened and purposeful.

If we feel inhibited or self-conscious about modeling, then we should practice in private, maybe with the help of a mirror for physical modeling and a tape recorder for aural modeling. In a very real sense, teaching is performing, and, like performance skills, teaching skills require practice! Another technique is to encourage more nonverbal participation from our students, particularly in the areas of physical and aural communication. We should explore our repertoire of sounds and neutral or nonsense syllables in terms of range, variety, and expressiveness. For example, can we produce explosive, percussive, sustained, and detached sounds with ease? Can we articulate different rhythmic patterns at different tempi? Can we syllabize inner voices as well as the obvious melodies, and so forth? If we can do these kinds of things, then our aural imaginations are likely to be lively and helpful in the teaching process.

If we choose to model music, then we need to be confident and clear in our intent. After all, a few measures of music may contain large amounts of information. Inadvertently, the student may be listening to something other than what is intended. Therefore it makes sense to keep musical modeling brief and specific so that students will focus on what is intended for them to hear.

The question of congruency between verbal and nonverbal behaviors has been addressed in chapter 4. Suffice it to say here that incongruities do arise quite easily. ("Do what I say and not what I do.") Is there a dull expression on our face when we speak of excitement in the music? Is there tension evident all over our body as we urge a more relaxed sound? Is there weakness in our hands and arms as we ask for strength of sound? Is there poor posture on the podium as we tell students to sit tall and breathe properly? Clearly the impact of our teaching can be significantly heightened if we increase the degree of congruency between verbal and nonverbal strategies. (See figure 7 in chapter 4 for an example of an evaluative checklist for nonverbal behaviors that can be used by observers, or by teachers themselves in evaluating recordings of their teaching efforts.)

Teaching-Style Flexibility

One major concern when we evaluate our music teaching effectiveness has to do with flexibility—the extent to which we can change or modify our teaching styles to meet the needs of individual students or different groups of students. Because we have delineated three primary vocabularies, three nonverbal options, and three basic areas of musical concern for diagnoses, we have the possibility of nine interacting variables. They may be represented diagrammatically, as in figure 18.

When we examine our music teaching, we may find a predominance of certain groupings or style profiles such as Technical Diagnosis-Professional Vocabulary-Physical Modeling, or Expressive Diagnosis-Musical Modeling-Experiential Vocabulary; but we should not assume that these are the best combinations of strategies, or that these are even desirable strategies. With experimentation we may find a combination of Conceptual Diagnosis-Experiential Vocabulary and Musical Modeling, or Expressive Diagnosis-Professional Vocabulary-Physical Modeling to be more effective, depending on the needs of particular students. The greater the repertoire of behaviors teachers have available at any given time, the more professionally competent they are likely to become. This is not to say they will employ all of these behaviors and combinations of behaviors at any given time; but, rather, if they are aware of the extensive range of choices available to them, they are more likely to select the most appropriate and effective behaviors.

> We have all experienced different teaching styles from time to time. Try to recall a style that was particularly effective for you.

Figure 18 Interacting Variables for Teaching Flexibility

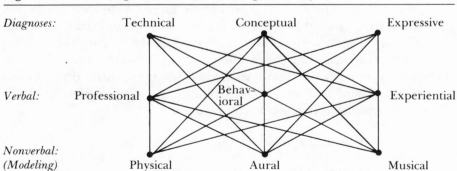

| *Diagnoses:* | Technical | Conceptual | Expressive |

| *Verbal:* | Professional | Behav-ioral | Experiential |

| *Nonverbal:* (Modeling) | Physical | Aural | Musical |

What in your estimation were some of the factors that contributed to that success? You might also consider a style that produced a negative response and isolate the reasons for that reaction.

Event Flow and Character

This area of evaluation has to do with the focus and flow rate of events within a lesson. Some of us are really high-powered generators in front of a class. We may diagnose a thousand different concerns in rapid succession. We may bombard our students with vivid vocabularies and fill the room with nonverbals! But there is a danger that both teacher and students might emerge dazed, exhausted, and confused from this kind of experience. Another alternative that is not recommended develops when we focus on one concern for protracted periods of time with minimal verbal or nonverbal behaviors. In other words, the lesson becomes characterized by the "let's do it again" syndrome, in the hope that the performance might improve. In fact, there is usually a perceptible increase in boredom and disappointment as the lesson proceeds. Here again the teacher and students may well emerge frustrated by the experience.

A lesson needs to shift focus from time to time as new concerns are diagnosed. Similarly, teaching strategies need a fluidity about them so that students are not exposed to static or totally predictable models. The basic qualities of an engaging lesson closely parallel those of an engaging piece of music. Sometimes we project too much too quickly while at other times we do just the reverse. We need to develop considerable and constant sensitivity to the degree of student involvement and absorption, and we need to be prepared to adjust the pace and character of our teaching behaviors accordingly. Again, regular evaluation of tapes of our teaching is called for.

Related to all this is the fact that sometimes teachers spend too little class or rehearsal time on teaching-learning activities and too much on discipline or business matters such as handing out and collecting music, planning fundraisers and trips, checking instruments or uniforms, and other housekeeping chores. A central focus for evaluation here should be on what is termed "engaged time" or "time on task." In other words, how effective is the teacher in maximizing the amount of time that the students are effectively engaged in the learning experiences at hand vis-à-vis disengaged time due to confusion, boredom, lack of efficient planning, organization, or discipline, and excessive housekeeping business?

What are some of the factors that might influence the rate of change in events in a music classroom? Under what circumstances would you recommend a rapid flow of events? When would you consciously limit diagnoses? When would you limit verbal in favor of nonverbal behavior, and vice versa? What are some ways you can maximize students' "on task" time?

Linkage

The final area for consideration in evaluating teacher effectiveness has to do with what might be called linkage. Our ability to perceive and respond to relationships is fundamental to the learning process. Nevertheless, it is an ability that appears to vary enormously from person to person. Some people are able to make connections between all kinds of apparently unrelated events while others find such a task impossibly complex. Some teachers are particularly skilled in teaching for linkage; they make consistent efforts to bridge phenomena so that students can develop significant relationships and build more meaningful wholes.

In the music class, educational linkage might have to do with a diagnosed concern relating technical modifications in bowing and improved violin tone quality. Such linkage may be accomplished through use of professional vocabulary and/or musical modeling. For another example, we might have a conceptual concern with phrasing linked to more subtle expressiveness via a shared experiential vocabulary and aural modeling. More generally we may want to link what we think with what we hear and what we feel. We may want to link what we perceive with what we hear and what we feel. We may want to link what we perceive with how we respond, or link musical memory with musical imagination. In the larger arena, we may want to link musical processes and experiences with life processes and experiences by means of experiential vocabulary and dialogue.

If we think about our teaching very carefully, we will undoubtedly discover endless opportunities to teach for linkage. Many opportunities are probably overlooked in the interest of more immediate or more simple goals, but we must remember that linkage is a vital factor in the development of meaning and value, and it must therefore hold a high priority for teaching effectiveness and for teacher evaluation.

Obviously teaching is a highly complex enterprise, and we must review and assess our efforts frequently to grow in effectiveness. Figure 19 is designed as an example of an analytic aid for the evaluation of teaching styles. The chart or selected parts of it can be used by classroom or lesson observers, or by teachers themselves in reviewing videotapes of their work.

Can you think of examples apart from music where increased linkage has increased meaning and significance for you? Can you think of a musical example? Listen to a recorded excerpt and compare the kinds of linkage that students in the class ex-

Figure 19 A Chart for Use in the Observation and Evaluation of Teaching Styles

TEACHER: STUDENT–*CLASS*:   GRADE: RECORDER: DATE:

	PROFESSIONAL VOCABULARY			EXPERIENTIAL VOCABULARY		BEHAVIORAL VOCABULARY			MODELLING			OTHER			
	Physical	Formal	Aesthetic	Image	Metaphor	Life Analog	Think	Feel	Share	Physical	Aural	Musical	Management	Teacher Music	Student Music	Student Question	Student Statement
1																
2																
3																
4																
5																
6																
7																
8																
9																
10																
11																
12																
13																
14																
15																
16																
17																
18																
19																
20																

1. The number of minutes into the observation-evaluation are indicated in the left hand column.

2. A "Q" or an "S" may be placed in the vocabulary columns to indicate whether the teacher asks a question or makes a statement.

3. The management column can indicate nonmusical behaviors related to discipline or routine matters.

4. Check the "Teacher Music" column when the teacher in NOT intentionally providing a musical model, i.e., the teacher may simply be playing along with or accompanying the student.

5. Analyze the data vertically and horizontally to determine the frequencies of behaviors and the relationships among behaviors. These might include the following:
   (a) numbers and types of questions
   (b) speed, complexity, and areas of diagnosis
   (c) relationships between verbal and nonverbal behaviors
   (d) range of vocabulary usage
   (e) relationships between different vocabularies
   (f) student input
   (g) time devoted to management procedures
   (h) flexibility of teaching style

perience. To what extent does the sharing increase the intensity
and/or quality of your experiences with repeated hearings?

PROGRAM EVALUATION

From time to time we are asked to make assessments and value judgments about the music programs with which we are associated. The
criteria for making such judgments may not always be clear. Our
conclusions may be based on personalities, facilities, awards, peers,
equipment, the degree of challenge or fun associated with the program, or some other criteria, but in order to do justice to program
evaluation, we need to develop a comprehensive and systematic approach. It should include observations and assessments concerning:
(1) the appropriateness of the principles, aims, objectives, and experiences that constitute the program; (2) the degree of support that
is available for meeting the stated principles, aims, objectives, and
experiences; (3) the degree of congruence between teacher behaviors
and the stated principles, aims, objectives, and experiences; and (4)
the degree of student progress that is attributable to the program's
principles, aims, objectives, and experiences. We shall consider each
of these criteria in turn.

Appropriateness of Principles, Aims, Objectives, and Experiences

There are two primary areas for consideration here: community
expectations and professional expectations. On the one hand, it is
reasonable to assume that goals (the term used here in the generic
sense to encompass principles, aims, objectives, and experiences) for
a particular program will be determined at least in part by the expectations of the particular community in which the program resides.
It is also reasonable to assume that the administrators and teachers
involved in a program will influence goal development based on their
professional training and expertise. Therefore, effective efforts must
be made to synchronize community and professional expectations.
Without continuous communication and synchronization each group
is likely to accuse the other of inappropriate behaviors, subgroups in
the school will feel ignored, or subgroups in the community will feel
ill-served, and, inevitably, progress toward goal achievement will be
undermined.

Reflect on your own high school music program. To what extent
did the goals of that program represent professional and community interests? If only one of these interest groups had been
represented how would that have affected the program?

In view of the varied and complex functions music now serves in our communities, expectations for music in education are by no means clear. Interested parents and students are often confused about why music should be in the curriculum and what particular educational goals it should serve. There is an urgent and ongoing need for music teachers to make their intent known as clearly as possible. The profession needs to communicate with parents and students in ways that are clear, open, and relevant. We hope the material in this book will help clarify what in fact needs to be communicated, and thereby facilitate the process.

If your school administrators appeared to be confused about the role of music in your school and in your community, what would you do to help resolve the problem?

Confusion and even disillusionment often develop when there is notable disparity between professional and community expectations. Perhaps the most vivid examples of such disparity occur within large inner city programs where professional expectations sometimes appear to have little in common with community expectations. However, examples also occur within a single school or a small system simply because expectations are confused or changing at different rates for different interest groups.

If there is to be any movement toward preventing or resolving these kinds of problems, it is most likely to come about through the planning process and by encouraging input at different levels within that process. For example, professional expectations may be most sharply focused at the experience level of planning, but community expectations can best be articulated at the principle or aim level of planning. The premise is that community input should be sought at general levels of planning whereas professional input should become more significant at specific levels. A disparity of expectations is less likely to arise if these guidelines are known to all concerned, and followed. Accordingly, principles, aims, and experiences are more likely to be deemed appropriate by all parties, and progress toward their achievement can be reasonably expected.

Questionnaires and opinion-assessment instruments can provide a good source of evaluative feedback. Timely use of such techniques can reveal valuable information about community and professional expectations, their congruity or incongruity, the degree to which they are being met, as well as about the effectiveness of the communication process itself.

Degree of Support

If a commitment has been made toward commonly held goals, then there must also be a tangible measure of support to achieve these goals. Principles, aims, and experiences will be little more than idle dreams unless they are supported with a qualified faculty, adequate facilities, instruments, materials, a reasonable schedule, a student group or class size that is related to function, and so forth. If this kind of tangible support is not forthcoming, then goals must be modified until they are realistic. The parties who have input into determining the goals of a program certainly should be fully informed and acquainted with any goal-support anomalies or incongruities because they may be able to help remedy such situations. Many music programs have parent groups or other community support organizations that, given the opportunity, can go well beyond simple fund raising activities to provide valuable help and insight in the planning and decision-making process, and thus be more effective in the program support process as well.

> Compare the kinds of support that were made available for your school programs. How can you account for the disparity between schools? What were some of the results, tangible and intangible, that you would attribute to the degree of program support?

If program planning has been a cooperative venture with a real concern for goal appropriateness, then it is reasonable to assume that funding and support also will be a cooperative venture. An involved community that has input into a program, is excited by a program, and can see the benefits of a program is most likely to support its continuance and expansion.

Unfortunately many music teachers feel isolated from the educational mainstream. They may be highly skilled music teachers and dedicated to the instructional task at hand, but their perception of their position is confined to the classroom or rehearsal room. This can be a self-defeating attitude in a world that is more broadly oriented. Music teachers need the support of their colleagues and their administrators as well as the community of students, parents, and other concerned citizens. That support is most likely to be forthcoming when music teachers become part of the basic educational structure and the total education scene, when they reach out to interact with other aspects of school and community programs. That kind of interaction and visibility provides opportunities for program evaluation and feedback, discussion, clarification, stimulation, and ultimately for the kind of broad support base we all need.

Degree of Congruence

We cannot evelute a music program without examining teacher behaviors and the extent to which those behaviors are congruent with the stated principles, aims, and experiences of the program. Incongruities may arise at many points and in many ways within a program. For example: an aim for a choral program may stress experience with a comprehensive range of literature, but in fact the teacher utilizes music from only one or two stylistic periods. A principle may stress opportunities for creative musical experiences, but the teacher emphasizes imitation. A principle may stress the importance of aesthetic awareness, but the teaching strategies do not employ a professional aesthetic vocabulary nor an experiential vocabulary. We may find some aspect of planning that stresses the importance of imaginative or feelingful response, but in fact most frequently students are being required to think logically, analytically, and deductively.

Examine the goals of some published curriculum guides and discuss the kinds of teacher behaviors these goals imply to you.

Some incongruities arise without a teacher's knowledge; they slip into day-to-day strategies or perhaps they have been part of a teacher's professional preparation. In any event, inconsistencies between stated goals and methodologies can soon appear, particularly if a teacher enters a new program and is not alert to all aspects of the situation. A teacher may be attracted to a new idea at an in-service workshop, perhaps some new literature or some new recordings. It is easy to adopt them on the spot without first determining if they are in line with program goals, sequences, and priorities. We may think that the new idea or the new methodology will excite the students or even "turn them around," and indeed that may in fact happen; but a series of innovations that are peripheral or quite external to a program's goals will ultimately confuse and detract from its effectiveness.

There are already many references in this text to the importance of flexibility of teaching style as it involves diagnostic, verbal, and nonverbal behaviors. Particular teaching styles and strategies are not in themselves good or bad. Their effectiveness can only be evaluated in relation to program goals, and to student progress toward achieving those goals. By focusing on the degree of congruence between teacher behaviors and program goals, we are taking into account two very significant factors or components that influence the relative success or failure of a music program. If there is incongruity between these components, the program can have only limited success. For example, a teacher with a wonderfully flexible teaching style will still be severely handicapped working in a program which, from that teacher's viewpoint, has inappropriate goals. Similarly, a program that has been developed cooperatively from a broad base of professional and community goal input is still apt to founder if the teaching styles employed in it are inflexible or narrow. Therefore, it is vitally important that decisions about teaching and program effectiveness be made in relation to other variables that directly impinge on that effectiveness. It should also be obvious that the amount of support that teachers receive in a program will have a direct bearing on teacher and program effectiveness, and this must be considered along with congruency in the evaluative process. For example, a teacher who has been struggling in an inner city school with minimal or outmoded facilities and equipment may be identified as an inferior teacher or a "burnout." However, if the same person were able to teach in an affluent suburban school he or she might be considered an effective or even superior teacher.

Summarizing, the teacher and the program are viewed as vital, intertwined links in the educational enterprise. Their evaluation must relate to their degree of congruity, to the level of support they enjoy, and to the appropriateness of their goals and goal development procedures.

> Think of one of the best music teachers you have ever had and one of the least effective. Now imagine them trading their teaching situations. How might that have affected your estimation of their impact?

Degree of Student Progress

Here again it is easy to be mistaken about the quality of a music program unless we view the total scene carefully. One or two outstanding students do not necessarily indicate a superior program. A closer inspection may reveal that those students received a significant amount of their instruction outside the program. Nor should we be quick to assume that large numbers of participants in a program necessarily indicate the inherent value of a program. Indeed, music may offer a more attractive alternative than other "undesirable" choices, or numbers may be high because achievement is low and expectations are minimal, or because "A" grades are easy to come by. For whatever reasons, quantity in and of itself does not necessarily indicate quality.

In evaluating the previous component of program effectiveness we took into account the degree of congruency between teacher behaviors and stated goals. The same is true for evaluating the student component of program effectiveness. We need to determine the extent to which student needs and student behaviors are congruent with the stated goals.

> Were you aware of the goals of your high school music program? Are you aware of the goals in your current program? If you had the opportunity to help develop a statement of goals for your current program, would you wish to do so? What advantages and disadvantages would you anticipate in being involved? Would it be a motivational experience? In what sense?

If program goals have been carefully stated, the importance of individual differences will be recognized. In other words, there will be a range of different expectations to provide for different students. Some will be expected to exhibit a wide range of musical behaviors and achieve a high level of intensity within their musical experiences. For others, the range and intensity of the behaviors may be less, based on their individual abilities, interests, and prior experience. By the same token, an enhanced behavior range and intensity level need not be achieved via the same route for all students. Some will be producers, some mainly consumers, and some will be both. Some will become interested in music history or theory and composition while others will concentrate on musical performance or listening.

If the rate of student progress toward goal achievement leaves something to be desired, then one needs to examine: (1) the students' perceptions of the stated goals; (2) the students' assessments of the appropriateness of the goals; and (3) the students' assessments of the appropriateness of the experiences developed to achieve those goals. If there is any notable degree of confusion or incongruity among program goals or between teacher and student perceptions of those goals, then progress toward goal achievement is likely to be inhibited. Students need to know where they are going, why they are going there, and how they are going to get there. Many times music students are confused on all three counts, generally because we have not allowed for timely and effective evaluative feedback and communication concerning those points.

How would you respond to these three basic questions: What role is music going to play in your life? Why? What do you have to do to prepare for it? Suggest how you would help your students consider these matters.

If we continue to seek relationships between man, music, and education, answers to such basic questions will be found. But this implies an extension of professional focus from producing and consuming music to an increasing awareness of what is, what could, and what should be happening to the students while the production or consumption of music is in progress. If students are given the opportunity and encouragement to develop personally and functionally with music, it seems likely that their commitment to it will deepen, and, in turn, program quality will be enhanced.

Conclusion

Program evaluation will not attain its true potential and value unless those involved in the process are willing and able to communicate effectively and modify certain aspects of the program—to implement change where and when it is found desirable. If we accept the view that program evaluation is or should be an ongoing process, then perhaps it is easier to accept change. If, on the other hand, program evaluation is viewed as only an occasional responsibility, it can become simply a bothersome isolated event, or alternatively something to be treated less than seriously.

Unlike some professions, music education has not yet been extensively challenged to make dramatic changes as a result of expanding technology. Ours is a curricular area that has been characterized by occasional new devices and methodologies, most of which have done little to change underlying principles and assumptions. That time may be past and we may have to address more current and fundamental issues such as what are the potential appeals, the proper roles, and the priority functions of music in a new century and in a global society? Can music provide a vital link between our internal and external worlds, between our personal and social lives? Can it provide a structure to assist self-knowledge and self-fulfillment? Can music really educate?

To gain recognition as a "basic," music programs will need to be able to undergo evaluation on a basis much more comprehensive than one of performance ratings or numbers of enrollees. Today's evaluation concerns must center on the more fundamental ability of music programs to facilitate progressive, qualitative, man-music interactions leading to the kinds of personal caring and social sharing that advance human development. Programs need to be evaluated in terms of their ability to foster thoughtful, feelingful, and sharing behaviors and lifestyles in which music is employed to its full potential, in a multitude of ways, to fulfill basic human needs and enhance the human condition. These are our professional responsibilities, the real bases of our evaluation, and of our value.

EXTENSIONS

Statements

1. "The experiences the pupils have when confronting music are the very center of the music curriculum. It is only here that actual learning can take place. What the students do during a confrontation with music is the most important concern of a curriculum evaluator." Sidnell, Robert, *Building Instructional Programs in Music Education* (Englewood Cliffs, N.J.: Prentice-Hall, 1973), p. 138.

2. "There are many areas of human behavior and of learning that intelligence does not encompass. Recent research indicates that musicality is at least as complex as intelligence." Colwell, Richard, *The Evaluation of Music Teaching and Learning* (Englewood Cliffs, N.J.: Prentice-Hall, 1970), p. 71.

3. "Assessment techniques do not only measure learning; they also affect it. How students perceive assessment devices and what they learn from the employment of such devices must be matters of vital concern in the selection of evaluative instruments." Combs, Arthur W., *Educational Accountability: Beyond Behavioral Objectives* (Washington: Association for Supervision and Curriculum Development, 1972), p. 3.

4. "Evaluation is the process of determining the extent to which the objectives of an educational enterprise have been attained. It involves three steps: (1) the identification, formulation and validation of objectives; (2) the collection of data relevant to status in relation to those objectives; (3) the interpretation of the data collected." Leonhard, Charles, and House, Robert W., *Foundations and Principles of Music Education* (New York: McGraw-Hill, 1972), p. 390.

5. "Management programs, accountability and test scores are what schools are about today and children know it. They have to produce or else. This pressure may be good for many students, but it is bound to be bad for those who can't keep up." Elkind, David, *The Hurried Child: Growing Up Too Fast Too Soon* (Reading, Mass.: Addison-Wesley, 1981), p. 55.

Questions and Suggestions

1. Define and discuss the nature of musical aptitude as a developing concept in music education. Cite any recent tests or studies that have contributed to your understanding of the concept and explore their practical implications for music education.

2. We have argued that experience involves both perception and response, but in music education we have tended to concentrate on perception rather than response. Why do you think this has been so? Can you think about and develop some new techniques that may more adequately evaluate musical response?

3. List the categories or areas that are important when developing evaluation profiles of your students' musical progress.

4. If you wished to evaluate a child's potential for success in musical performance, what kinds of information would you try to accumulate? Why?

5. Create three test items that will in your opinion evaluate a student's musical imagination.

6. Develop a series of five items for a test of musical aptitude. How would these items differ if they were to appear in a test of musical achievement, a test of musical imagination, or a test of musical creativity?

7. Reflect on the music evaluations you received in school. If grades were given, were you acquainted with the criteria for their determination? On what bases would you have liked to have been evaluated?

8. A constant concern facing all teachers has to do with the choice of evaluating amount of effort, amount of achievement, or both. Why might you select one option rather than another?

9. Discuss the concept of "intensity" as a positive or negative force in life. Then discuss it as a positive or negative artistic or educational force. Can quality really be achieved without intensity? What factors in your

own life determine whether intensity produces negative or positive results?

10. If evaluation is to involve range and intensity of musical behaviors, what are the implications for planning and teaching? What are some of the things you would expect to observe in a music program that places high value on the range and intensity of student musical experiences?

11. Experiencing music involves a selective process because we simply cannot perceive everything that is happening from moment to moment. Nor can we respond to everything we are perceiving, so we discriminate and make choices. It is the nature of those choices that lies at the heart of music education because they may be based on ignorance or on understanding. Discuss in detail with your colleagues how they experience a particular musical event and evaluate one another's range of choices.

12. Locate a standardized test that you would like to utilize for diagnostic purposes. Discuss why you selected that particular test.

13. Which of the three possible areas of expressive, conceptual, or technical concerns do you most naturally diagnose in your own performances? Is that an area of weakness or strength in your mind? Have you noticed the emphasis of your diagnosis shifting according to your teacher's particular emphasis?

14. Consider the importance of nonverbal behavior in your own music education. Did your teacher provide frequent musical or aural modeling? How valuable was this teaching behavior to your own development as a musician? Do you think teachers of some instruments should model more frequently than others? Why?

15. Give some examples of how flexibility in teaching styles can be demonstrated and evaluated in a classroom situation.

16. Can you recall emerging from a music class or lesson feeling quite hopeless and wondering if it was worth your while continuing to study music? Try to analyze the reasons that produced that state of mind. What does this tell you about self-concept and one's evaluation of personal progress? If you had been the teacher, what could you have done to preclude such a feeling of hopelessness?

17. Think about some of your own music teachers and how you evaluated them. Was it on the basis of musical competence, personality, teaching effectiveness, or popularity? How would *you* like to be evaluated by your students?

18. Explain the criteria you would employ and the procedures you would follow in evaluating a high school music program of your choice.

19. Try to locate evidence that may demonstrate how the goals of a music education program have been influenced by the community that it serves. What are some of the actions you would take in a new music teaching situation so that you might draw the community and the music program more closely together? How would you evaluate your progress in this endeavor?

20. Interview two music teachers representing different levels of the school

system and try to determine the adequacy of the support they receive. Is the support generous, realistic, minimal, or totally inadequate? What are the bases and criteria for your evaluation and conclusion?

21. Examine music test items from the National Assessment of Educational Progress (see reference in readings list). Which of those aspects of music education emphasized in this text are addressed by NAEP test items and which are not? Which NAEP testing approaches seem most useful for some of your evaluation purposes as a music educator?

22. In what ways would you like to see current concepts of evaluation in music education changed during the next decade? If evaluation emphases were to be changed, how would teaching practices be affected?

REFERENCES AND READINGS

Borich, Gary D., and Madden, Susan K. *Evaluating Classroom Instruction.* Menlo Park, Calif.: Addison-Wesley, 1977.

Centra, John A. *Determining Faculty Effectiveness.* San Francisco: Jossey-Bass, 1980.

Colwell, Richard. *The Evaluation of Music Teaching and Learning.* Englewood Cliffs, N.J.: Prentice-Hall, 1970.

Ecker, David W.; Johnson, Thomas J.; and Kaelin, Eugene F. "Aesthetic Inquiry." *Review of Educational Research,* December 1969, vol. 39, no. 5, pp. 577–92.

Guba, Egon G. "Naturalistic Inquiry." *Improving Human Performance Quarterly,* 1979, vol. 8, pp. 268–76.

Guba, Egon G. "Toward a Methodology of Naturalistic Inquiry in Educational Evaluation." In *CSE Monograph Series in Evaluation, No. 8.* Los Angeles: Center for the Study of Evaluation, UCLA, 1978.

Guba, Egon G., and Lincoln, Yvonna S. *Effective Evaluation: Improving the Usefulness of Evaluation Results Through Responsive and Naturalistic Approaches.* San Francisco: Jossey-Bass, 1981.

Kaplan, Max. *Foundations and Frontiers of Music Education.* New York: Holt, Rinehart and Winston, 1966, ch. 5.

Kerlinger, Fred N. *Foundations of Behavioral Research: Educational and Psychological Inquiry.* New York: Holt, Rinehart and Winston, 1965.

Knieter, Gerard L., and Stalling, Jane, eds. *The Teaching Process and Arts and Aesthetics.* St. Louis: CEMREL, 1979.

Kwalwasser, Jacob. *Exploring the Musical Mind.* New York: Coleman-Ross Co., 1955.

Lehman, Paul R. *Tests and Measurements in Music.* Englewood Cliffs, N.J.: Prentice-Hall, 1968.

Leonhard, Charles. "Evaluation in Music Education." In *Basic Concepts in Music Education.* Chicago: National Society for the Study of Education, 57th Yearbook, 1958.

Madeja, Stanley S., ed. *The Arts, Cognition and Basic Skills.* St. Louis: CEMREL, 1978.

Mursell, James L. *Music Education Principles and Programs.* Morristown, N.J.: Silver Burdett Co., 1956.

Music Educators National Conference (MENC). *Documentary Report of the Ann Arbor Symposium.* Reston, Va.: MENC, 1981.

Music Educators National Conference (MENC). *The School Music Program: Description and Standards.* Vienna, Va.: MENC, 1974.

National Assessment of Educational Progress (NAEP). *Music 1971–79: Results from the Second National Music Assessment,* no. 10-MU-01. Denver: NAEP, November 1981.

National Assessment of Educational Progress (NAEP). *The Second Assessment of Music, 1978–79: Released Exercise Set,* no. 10-MU-25. Denver: NAEP, April 1980.

Phelps, Roger P. *A Guide to Research in Music Education.* Metuchen. N.J.: Scarecrow Press, 1980.

Raths, L.; Harmin, M.; and Simon, S. *Values and Teaching.* Columbus, Ohio: Charles E. Merrill Books, 1966.

Ross, Jerrold L. "Teacher Education for AGE Programs." *The Music Educators Journal,* January 1978, pp. 81–83.

Silver, M. *Values Education.* Washington: National Education Association, 1976.

Simon, S.; Howe, L.; and Kirschenbaum, H. *Values Clarification, A Handbook of Practical Strategies for Teachers and Students.* New York: Hart Publishing Co., 1972.

Thorndike, Robert, and Hagan, Elizabeth. *Measurement and Evaluation in Psychology and Education.* New York: John Wiley and Sons, 1969.

Weyland, Rudolph H. *A Guide to Effective Music Supervision: Part IV.* Dubuque, Iowa: Wm. C. Brown Co., 1960.

Whybrew, William E. *Measurement and Evaluation in Music.* Dubuque, Iowa: Wm. C. Brown, 1971.

Index